# How to Build a Successful Career

# *How to Build a Successful Career*

## *How to Stop Job-Hunting and Start Career-Building*

# *ALAN JONES*

Hutchinson
Business
Books

First published in 1991 by Business Books Limited
An imprint of Random Century Limited
20 Vauxhall Bridge Road, London SW1V 2SA

Random Century Australia (Pty) Limited
20 Alfred Street, Milsons Point, Sydney
New South Wales 2061, Australia

Random Century New Zealand Limited
9–11 Rothwell Avenue, Albany, Glenfield
Auckland 10, New Zealand

Century Hutchinson South Africa (Pty) Limited
PO Box 337, Bergvlei 2012, South Africa

Set in Garamond and Univers by Servis Filmsetting Ltd

Printed and bound in Great Britain by
The Guernsey Press Co. Ltd, Guernsey, Channel Islands

British Library Cataloguing in Publication Data
Jones, Alan
    How to build a successful career: how to stop job-hunting and start
career-building
    1. Job hunting
    I. Title
    650.14

ISBN 0-09-174662-0

# CONTENTS

## PART THREE: HOW TO FIND THE RIGHT JOB

# ACKNOWLEDGMENTS

Special thanks to Mike Potter for his professional advice and to Jeff Roberts for providing the initial inspiration.

# INTRODUCTION

You have got to kiss a lot of frogs to find a prince. In career terms, many people never find their prince and give up kissing frogs altogether: they grab the first frog that kisses *them* and refuse to let go. People for whom a job is no more than a necessary evil and simply a means to an end may not be very concerned about this – but then they are unlikely to pick up this book. But those who have a frog of a job and yearn for something better will want to know what can be done about it. This book is for those of you *whose careers are not taking you to where you want to be.*

Personal career management is a relatively new concept. Until fairly recently, voluntarily changing employers to fulfil personal career ambitions was regarded as an option open only to those 'high flyers' headhunted by other employers. Indeed, changing your employer in this way is even now perceived by some as being no more than idiosyncratic behaviour.

This perception has arisen through ignorance of the distinction between a **job** and a **career**, and through confusion regarding the *ownership* of each. For their part, employers naturally want to attract and retain those whom they regard as 'quality people'. To attract applicants they will advertise themselves and their jobs in the best possible light. To retain them they will espouse to manage the employees' career development within the organization. As employees we are often happy to go along with the idea – how reassuring to believe that others will manage our career development!

Part 1 will explore this phenomenon and look at the reasons, real or imagined, why we are prepared to accept career inertia and resist change, even when we are in the throes of a severe career menopause. It will explain why it is that an employer can only manage your career within strictly defined parameters. It will demonstrate that, from your employer's point of view, your career needs will *always* be subordinate to other factors and that the best way to reach your career objectives is through taking on the responsibility of managing your own career.

In Part 2 the options will be explored. If your career

menopause is severe enough it may require a life change even more radical than just getting a better job. Change presents opportunities and this could be an ideal opportunity for you to take a completely different course. It is certainly an opportunity to at least consider the possibilities of doing so, although most readers will probably discover that the best way ahead is to find a better job with a new employer.

Part 3 provides the practical means to pursue this option. Getting the *right* job is a skill in itself and conducting an effective job search is not for the faint-hearted. There is practical advice on every stage of the job search, from analyzing the job market right through to negotiating salary. This advice is based upon the experiences of thousands of job-seekers I have counselled during the last ten years. Almost without exception those who achieved the greatest degree of success displayed a combination of the four most essential qualities: tactics, timing, technique and tenacity.

It really is within your power to turn your frog into a prince, so go ahead and discover *why* and *how* it should be done. But a word of warning – your prince, once found, always has the potential to turn back into a frog. Personal career management is an ongoing process.

# Part One

# Whose Career is it Anyway?

# CHAPTER ONE

## Diagnosing the Problem

On balance, having a job – any job – is preferable to having no job at all, unless the 'income' (both in financial and fulfilment terms) from it is so derisory as to destroy the incentive to work.

However, given that we can expect to spend a third of our allotted time span in the workplace, we really do owe it to ourselves to choose jobs which we (and not necessarily other people) define as being the *right* jobs for us. Most of us at some time find ourselves in the wrong job. This is not always a cause for alarm, particularly if what preceded it was good and what is very likely to follow it is even better. Alarm bells should ring only if you have held a succession of wrong jobs and the future seems likely to promise more of the same. In this situation it is unlikely that you are following a meaningful career path at all, and the need to do something about the situation is certainly acute.

Typically, the 'Career Menopause' strikes between the ages of 35 and 55 and affects those who up until the onset of the Menopause had considered themselves to have been following an acceptable career path. After the age of 55 if the Career Menopause has not struck it is most unlikely to do so.

### What are the symptoms?

### Downturn in performance

This is not to be confused with constant poor performance which can be the result of innate lack of ability or inadequate training. But if you had previously been performing well then a gradual downturn in performance is a classic symptom of dissatisfaction.

We tend to be good at the jobs we are happy doing. In many jobs, we reach a point where we become so good that it becomes second nature, ceases to present a challenge and no longer allows us to innovate or inject anything new. We then cease to be happy and as a result performance suffers through lack of enthusiasm. We will also become unhappy once we realize that we have become as good at the job as we are ever going to get, which may be good enough but not earth-shatteringly so.

## Loss of job satisfaction

This symptom is rather more complex. How does one measure job satisfaction? It is impossible to quantify in any meaningful way. One thing more than any other which reinforces our feeling of having no job satisfaction is our perception that other people have lots of it. Peer envy is a natural part of the human condition ('every time a friend succeeds I die a little') but is no more than a sideshow to the real problem upon which you must focus your attention, ie that *you* have a job which gives no opportunity to show what you can really achieve, is not utilizing the best of your skills and which is very likely to drive you barking mad if you stick with it for much longer. This does not mean that it is in itself a *bad* job – many others might find it infinitely rewarding. But for you it is the *wrong* job. What did you achieve today? Was it *new*? Was it *fun*?

## Behavioural changes

Downturn in performance and loss of job satisfaction will inevitably lead to changes in behaviour. If you are in the midst of the Career Menopause, the odds are that your colleagues are finding you difficult to deal with. Examples of such changes are:

- Short temper
- Lower patience threshold
- An increasing tendency to *say* that you don't suffer fools gladly
- Refusal to admit mistakes
- Apportioning blame to others

- Verbal aggression
- Mischievousness
- Disruptive behaviour

Paranoia may lead to delusions of grandeur – telling people that you are too good for the job, to the extent that it no longer requires 100 per cent of your attention, coupled with an increasing belief that you are surrounded by incompetents. You may also suffer delusions of persecution – belief that a certain individual (line, senior or personnel manager) or group of individuals is scheming to put your career development on the back burner, or even to ease you out of the organization altogether.

Of course none of the above may be delusions at all. Perhaps you *are* too good for the job, you *are* surrounded by incompetents and they *really are* out to get you. If so then you are most certainly in the wrong job.

So here you are then, achieving little in the way of results for your employer, nothing for yourself in terms of job satisfaction and displaying all the signs of mental instability. Time for some positive action one would think. Time to grasp this particular nettle and take charge of your career – weigh up the options, identify the good jobs, go for them, improve the quality of your life, do something! And yet . . . and yet . . . you resist making the change. You erect barriers, deny that the problem exists and, even if you accept that there is a problem, pretend that now is not the time to make your move.

The result of all this is career inertia. This traditional tendency to overstay our welcome in a job is extremely common and damaging, both to our career progression and to our development as human beings. Lack of exposure to different stimuli is not conducive to producing well-rounded and free-thinking individuals (although some people seek, and find, compensations outside the workplace).

To overcome career inertia and unlock the door to the future we must first find the key. The key is to be found through understanding *why* we resist making the change even when the Career Menopause is severe enough to seriously damage our health. The rest of Part 1 is designed to help you find your personal key. We will look more closely at the reasons why we resist change so strongly, with particular emphasis on the relationship between employer and employee.

## A job or a career?

A career can be defined as 'a profession or occupation chosen as one's life's work'. The changing nature of work and our attitudes towards it over the past 20 years are beginning to render the word 'career' obsolete. It is alarming that many people believe they have a career when in reality they have had no more than a succession of different jobs. (This is not necessarily bad news, however, providing what they have achieved has come up to their expectations.) Most people's careers are not *planned*, at least not by the individuals themselves. Rather than being a forward-looking exercise, career-planning tends to be *backward-looking*, ie a career is merely something we look back on to see if we have had one, rather than *a vehicle for getting us to where we want to be*. Unfortunately, for many people where they want to be is anybody's guess.

A well-planned, progressive and rewarding career can be immensely satisfying, give you adequate monetary rewards and allow you to grow as a person. But a 'career' can also be a strait-jacket. It can restrict freedom of movement, stifle imagination and diminish the human spirit. Which description fits your career, and are you happy with it? Perhaps you didn't choose your career at all – it may have been chosen for you or it may even have chosen you.

The vital point for anyone interested in self-development is that a career should not be *inert* – to take you into the future it must be moving, or at least be capable of moving within a reasonable time frame. It is not unlike being stuck in a traffic jam. For anyone anxious to go places the frustration and stress of being strapped into an immovable vehicle can only be relieved by taking a course of *action*. The difference between being involuntarily stuck in the traffic and being frustrated in a career is that with the latter you have an alternative – change vehicles.

There is a common misconception that a good career is synonymous with *security* rather than with *progress*. As a result, we are often eager to hold on to the former – even if it means relinquishing the latter. Retirement is frequently seen as the natural conclusion to a career, and for the fortunate few who go out on a high note this is certainly true. But for the less fortunate (or less forward-looking), retirement is no more than an end to their particular prison sentence – their *career* may have ended 20 years earlier when they ceased to have any realistic hope of progressing further within their chosen vehicle of employment. The temptation to deny the truth of this will be great – few of us would care to admit that we have reached the end of the road – but, like it or not, a career ends when progress stops.

*Question to an employee:* 'What is a job?'
*Answer:* 'A job is a means of fulfilling my personal needs in terms of income, professional fulfilment, career progression and status.'

*Question to an employer:* 'What is a job?'
*Answer:* 'To me a job is a means of fulfilling the needs of the organization.'

Clearly, then, for both parties a job is a means of fulfilling needs – *but not the same needs*. Employers do not employ us in order that we might satisfy *our* needs. To them, *their* needs are of over-riding importance, and employing people is frequently (although less frequently) the only way to fulfil those needs.

The relationship between employer and employee is that of *buyer* and *seller*. A business transaction takes place whereby the buyer (employer) undertakes to pay an agreed sum of money to the seller (employee) who in turn undertakes to perform certain designated duties. The importance of this relationship is even more apparent when you are looking for a job, but for now it is only necessary to understand that the relationship may break down *when the needs of either party change.*

Perhaps the most dramatic breakdown can occur when, for various reasons, the employer no longer has a need for the job at all. In such circumstances, and unless other needs can be found for the employee to fulfil, the relationship will be terminated.

Of course, some employers set great store by the 'career progression' they can offer and this still forms the basis of their sales pitch to attract prospective employees, particularly on the university 'milk round'.

In practice – and whatever your abilities – the limits to your progression within such an organization must be defined by the *needs* of the organization. Once they have bought your skills, experience and qualifications, or invested in your potential by teaching you new skills, you will be used in such a way that their requirements can be met. This need not be as sinister as it sounds – if at the same time your needs are satisfied then the relationship will be harmonious. This is not a criticism of corporate policy but an observation on the way things are, for they can operate in no other way. Even for those of you 'locked in' to careers in the public sector, forward movement can only take place at a rate commensurate with the needs of that organization – employers with 'more chiefs than indians' have discovered this to their cost.

It is therefore dangerous to believe that your career needs will be automatically met by your employer. Such thinking is likely to be no more than an excuse for abdicating responsibility for your own career.

## The profit imperative

The *raison d'être* of private sector employers is not to employ people. Their major reason – usually their only reason – for being is to *make a profit*. Employing people is merely a means of making this happen, and a means which is becoming increasingly unnecessary. The old heavy industrial, labour-intensive organizations are all but gone. The technological revolution has given birth to the leisure revolution. *Change* is taking place and the companies which survive and go forward are those that have the ability, capacity and *vision* to accommodate these changes. To do so they must be receptive to change, and certain job functions will cease to become relevant to the needs of the organization. They may have little option but to make redundancies.

True redundancy can, then, only be defined as *a corporate reaction to changing events*. The prevalent myth is that only *unsuccessful* companies have to institute redundancies. The truth is that a successful company may sometimes be forced to introduce a redundancy programme in order to *stay* successful. Any company lacking the ability, vision or *will* to react quickly to changing events is in serious danger of sinking.

The relevance of this to you is that *jobs* become redundant and not *people*. Redundancy can strike any job at any time, even if that job is currently fulfilling a need and fulfilling it well.

## Don't stop the music

Envisage, for a moment, your career as a game of musical chairs. For much of the time the music is playing and exciting continual activity. People are moving meaningfully around the circuit in time to the music and progressing from one chair to another. There is a chair for everyone so all is peace and harmony. Then one day the MD (Master of the Dance) decides that one of the chairs is no longer necessary and removes it from the game. The music has stopped and someone is disappointed – you. Your chair has been removed and you now have to follow it out of the game, not because they don't want you anymore but because you have nowhere to sit. Your *chair* has become surplus to requirements – not you.

In truth, of course, you probably should shoulder some of the blame. Your eyes were open and you could see that the game was in progress. Perhaps you failed to see the warning signs that traditionally stop the music (see below), and could you not see that other chairs were being removed? Perhaps you became complacent because you were such a brilliant player? But when it really mattered you were too slow to react, and to all intents and purposes you may as well have been playing the game blindfold. If your *vision* had not been impaired the signs would have been clear and you could have chosen to remove yourself from the game in your own time and joined another game where the music was playing continuously.

If you *choose* to stay in a company where the music keeps stopping, such self-delusion will eventually catch up with you. If you *choose* to stick your head in the sand you will obviously have no vision.

But there *are* choices and there *are* alternatives. If you choose not to explore the alternatives you ought not to be surprised when events catch up with you. Just as redundancy to an employer is a corporate reaction to changing events, redundancy to an employee is, more often than not, *a failure in personal career management*.

## Factors which stop the music

Any one of the following factors is likely to initiate *change* within an organization. These in turn will frequently be cause for employers to review their needs in terms of jobs:

- Take-overs
- Mergers
- Excessively high interest rates
- New appointments to senior positions
- Low sales
- Fall off in production

- Changes in consumer tastes/fashion
- New/better products/services from competitors
- Weak management
- Government legislation

It is no coincidence that changes which *remove* career opportunities for some are exactly those which *create* opportunities for others. In Part 3 we will see how change or movement within an organization can be exploited by the alert job-seeker – but early identification of change can be equally valuable to those whose careers could be adversely affected by it.

If your job is in the private sector the actions of competitors can make your position vulnerable. For example, they may introduce a new product which virtually makes obsolete the one produced by your company, or at least makes it less competitive in the market place. If your employer decides to inject more resources into developing products to counter the new threat this may present job opportunities, but not necessarily for you. Alternatively, your employer may decide to withdraw from that market altogether, which is a change potentially more threatening to your career prospects.

If you have the vision to recognize the potential threat posed by a competing product you can make appropriate contingency plans, ie do the ground-work for a job-search campaign as outlined in Part 3 but stop short of actually applying for jobs until the situation becomes more clear. The initial remedial action by your employer may be a contraction of the workforce. Even if you are not an immediate casualty of such contractions, this should be a signal that for you the music is about to stop – you can assume that there will be a 'knock on' effect further up the line. Removing the foundations always tends to make the top a bit wobbly – an army reducing its complement of troops requires fewer officers.

Government legislation can certainly influence factors in both private and public sectors, the most obvious and visible being that of privatization. Imposing the profit ethos on hitherto publicly-owned organizations invariably requires a reduction in personnel. Privatization is, in career terms, an accident looking for somewhere to happen. Don't sit back and wait for it to arrive on your doorstep or hope that it will pass you by. If you allow inertia to reign supreme you may find yourself thrown into the job market with your colleagues who may be competing with you in that same market and at the same time – thus reducing your chances of finding the right job quickly.

Rising accommodation costs in the South East are currently motivating the Government to relocate the Civil Service into the regions, and private companies have been doing this for some time. Ironically, the Department of Employment sees itself as the forerunner of this move and is likely to transfer nine-tenths of its London-based jobs to the regions. In virtually all relocation moves the job-holder is given the option of following the job to its new location, but few take this up – a classic example of where the changing needs of the employer conflict with those of the employee. This is of course good news to anyone seeking work and residing in the favoured area, but it is a career watershed for those wanting to remain where they are. The message to anyone currently working in the South East of England is that they really ought to ask themselves how necessary it is for their employer to be there. If there is no specific business reason for being in the area, the issue of moving to a more cost-effective location will surely be addressed sooner or later.

Acquisitions, mergers and takeovers are other external factors which can force change upon an employer. The predator will be more inclined to use its existing staff in the running of the new acquisition (always assuming it intends to continue running it).

Internal changes can also stop the music. New appointments of senior personnel, ie of anyone with the power to influence policy or make decisions on business strategy, may well result in a 'streamlining' of operations which makes certain job functions obsolete or, more frequently, in the absorption of one person's job functions by other personnel ('Downsizing' is the American euphemism for such grand-scale music-stopping). Job 'security' is certainly affected by the relatively new, and growing, fashion of 'contracting out' certain services (ie giving an outside organization the responsibility of performing tasks previously done 'in house'). Catering, security, cleaning and marketing are the fore-runners of this trend but it is quickly expanding into other areas.

When any of the above changes are in their infancy or no more than a rumour within your organization, it can be difficult to predict with certainty whether the outcome will have an adverse effect on your position. At this stage the music is still playing and everyone has a chair to sit on. Any radical action on your part could well be precipitative and, even if your job is very likely to become redundant, you may not wish to pre-empt the situation by voluntarily moving on and foregoing any redundancy money you might be in line for. But to remain in control of events you must begin to develop a 'what if' scenario. Try to project forward and construct an action plan you can initiate if your 'worst case' scenario becomes reality. Consider your options, research your market place, identify possible alternative employers, up-date your CV. In short, have the mechanisms in place which will enable you to launch a job-search campaign *when* you want to launch it.

---

**Action checklist**

- Check for symptoms of Career Menopause
- Identify whether you have a career or a job
- Ask yourself if your needs are being satisfied
- Assess whether the music is likely to stop
- Develop an action plan

---

# CHAPTER TWO

## Finding the Key

### Escape from career complacency

Are you adding anything new to your 'career kitty' by undertaking new tasks, assuming new responsibilities and developing new skills which will enable you to achieve your next objective? Or is your career moribund to the point of stagnation, investing nothing for the future and contributing not one jot to your collection of transferable skills which would be attractive to another employer? Inability to give any meaningful answer to the above questions is a sure sign that your personal career management has been non-existent. In my experience, many job-seekers display a virtually total lack of awareness of their skills, achievements and the relevance of their experiences to the market place. When did you last look at your CV? A typical response to that question is along the lines of 'What CV – I've been working for the same company for 20 years, why do I need a CV?' This brings us to the first law of personal career management:

*Your CV is your passport to the future and you never know when you might be asked to travel, regardless of whether you want to go.*

There seems to be a general misunderstanding that the CV is merely something one hastily cobbles together when looking for a job. Wrong. It is *your* sales literature and should be permanently in existence and up-dated as your skills, experiences and achievements grow. It is an *inventory* of what you have done which in turn is a guide to potential buyers – an *indication* of what you can do.

Don't suffer from career complacency – if your CV is not growing then neither are you. Obviously, we cannot live our lives in a permanent state of motion. Most of us need an element of stability. An employee who is always moving on is not necessarily an attractive proposition to employers. But it is a question of *balance*. Employees who outstay their welcome far outnumber those who continually hop from one employer to another – we are not 'career gypsies' by nature.

Statistically, even if your career is moribund you still will not voluntarily move outside your company – you will stay in the hope that 'things will improve', you will have vague notions about the situation 'not being too bad' and will rationalize that you have a reasonable lifestyle so 'why rock the boat?' But, just as necessity is the mother of invention so inertia is the child of complacency. Only you can decide whether you are a 'sit back and see what turns up' or an 'I'd better do something' type of person.

In the past, career complacency has been more endemic and insidious in the public sector than in the corporate world. This is because the *needs* of public sector employers changed relatively little over time. The absence of competition and profit incentives lessened the danger of jobs becoming surplus to requirements and 'careers' being cut short by redundancies. This invited employees to become complacent about their careers because even if they reached a 'plateau' they had job security. This led to a kind of Faustian compromise which ultimately became self-destructive – careers were (and still are) cut short through lack of personal progress but the employee remained.

Times have changed. With university lecturers losing the coveted security of tenure, schools being locally managed and radical changes being mooted within the Civil Service/local government, the pendulum is swinging the other way. Whatever the problems of such changes, one certain outcome is that public sector employees will be given the freedom to manage their own careers – career responsibility will be handed back to its owner. Initially this freedom may not be gratefully received but ultimately it must be beneficial to both employer and employee. We are now more likely to see vastly increased freedom of movement in the workforce between private and public sectors – if for no other reason than that the two entities will be indistinguishable. Individuals caught up in this maelstrom of change may initially feel that their careers have been destroyed. But if a positive approach is adopted, far from being destroyed, such careers will in fact have been liberated.

## *The emotional hand-cuffs*

### A question of loyalty

Significant numbers of employees develop an emotional condition often referred to as 'loyalty to the company'. This in itself is harmless enough and develops out of a sense of camaraderie and the 'ethos' propagated by many companies themselves. When the music is playing this condition works very well for the company and gives a reassuring comfortable feel to its employees. Most of us like to feel that we belong and have an allegiance to something. Loyalty is after all a by-product of our need to love and be loved.

But does the concept really stand up to close examination? What do we really mean when we use the term 'the company'? We talk about 'the company' making a profit – but surely *people* make profits, not companies? A company is no more than an amorphous collection of people each of whom have one primary concern – *their* job. Does 'the company' exist at all other than as a vague concept in our minds which happens to act as a vehicle for our loyalty? Employees will frequently refer to 'the company' almost as if there exists some 'Father Christmas' type figure somewhere 'up there' looking after their interests. He doesn't exist – this ethos of paternalism is fostered quite deliberately to encourage loyalty and hence retention.

The acid test of loyalty is whether it works both ways. Even if there is some figurehead making reassuring noises about 'teamwork' and 'career development' it can only go so far – for when the music is playing loyalty is cheap. When corporate needs change and chairs are taken away the silence is deafening. Anyone reading this who has already been on the receiving end of redundancy will know the truth of it.

'Loyalty' in this sense is then an archaic concept and not founded on reality. It has more in common with serfdom and good old-fashioned subservience. When the chips are down it offers as much protection as an umbrella in a forest fire. The corporate bogeyman does exist! By all means work hard, be proud of the organization you represent and defend it against criticism – but resist using loyalty as your excuse for inaction when your career has ceased to progress.

## The myth of the caring company

If a company is incapable of the ultimate show of loyalty – keeping you in a job that is surplus to requirements – because everything must be subordinate to profit, how far can it go towards displaying a caring attitude to that amorphous group of people it comprises?

Well quite some way in fact. There are many examples of how employers have gone out of their way to support employees in, for example, moments of personal crisis. This will tend to happen even if such support requires some short-term financial sacrifice from the employer. There are a number of reasons why this is so. Firstly, the moral obligation to provide support is strong, although one hesitates to use the word 'moral' in the same sentence as 'business'. Morale is also a factor – if the company is not supportive of Joe in his efforts to overcome a personal problem, this can have a negative effect on morale within the workforce, the likely outcome of which is a reduction in productivity and hence profit.

The more 'caring' a company is the greater becomes its reputation as a 'good' company to work for. A few of the more forward-looking organizations are now investing in quite sophisticated EAPs (Employee Assistance Programmes) whereby external consultants are engaged to deal confidentially with a wide variety of personal crises encountered by employees eg financial, marital, legal, alcohol and work-related problems. The cost is borne by the company and the benefits are reduced absence through stress-related illness, attraction of staff and *lower staff turnover*. If the 1990s really is going to be the caring decade then EAPs will become an increasingly important recruitment and retention tool, particularly if employers are going to have to compete fiercely to attract people from a diminishing pool of human resources.

All of this is good news but 'lower staff turnover' by definition means that fewer employees will take it upon themselves to leave the organization to improve their lot, *even if their careers are stagnating*. 'The company has been very good to me in the past' is a common excuse for not taking control of one's own career and moving to more professionally (as opposed to emotionally) rewarding pastures. Willingness to submit to these emotional hand-cuffs is a significant failure in personal career management.

It is worth bearing in mind that many organizations deliberately propagate the philosophy of caring, sharing, the 'family' ethos, a 'band of brothers' that is good and rewarding to be part of, and even potentially harmful to be excluded from. It is also worth remembering that the Mafia is one of them.

## The security straitjacket

Retiring with a gold carriage clock (a gift heavy with irony) after 35 years service used to be a cause for celebration, and probably still is for those who survive the course. Security in a job used to be synonymous with success. Any thoughts on throwing up such a job, even to secure something better, were regarded as no more than eccentric behaviour. Advice from parents and careers officers to 'take a job with security' was only another way of saying 'let them handle your career' – and of course 'they' would, to a lesser or greater degree, for as we have seen the rate of your advancement is always subordinate to, and dictated by, *their* needs.

Things have now moved on apace. No longer should you be

content to surrender to others the management of your career, any more than you would let others dictate how you should spend your leisure time. There are many examples of people fulfilling themselves within, say, the Civil Service, achieving promotion and retiring after a most distinguished career. But for every one of them there are perhaps a hundred others, equally competent, but whose time has never come and is unlikely to. What of them? For them 'security' becomes the only reason for maintaining the status quo. They are locked in to a career which is going nowhere very slowly. The end result is that gradual slide into the Career Menopause which can have such a damaging effect not just on the individual but also on his or her family. Under these circumstances a career is secure in much the same way as a prison. Perhaps every contract of employment should carry a Government Health Warning: 'Security can seriously damage your prospects'.

## Overcoming the fear of risk

Some people never go on journeys on the premise that 'if you don't attempt anything you can't fail'. The paradox is that you won't achieve anything either so ultimate failure is assured. Lack of personal exposure to risk is popularly cloaked in that respectable veneer of 'contentment' and even self-confessed 'lack of ambition'. Lack of ambition is not a cardinal sin, providing it is honestly expressed, but so often it is no more than an excuse for inertia.

Personal career management is not 'risky'. To 'take a risk' is to proceed in an action without regard to the possibility of the danger involved. On that basis only the most stupid of racing drivers would tell you that he takes risks. Your career path is a journey and, like all journeys, to be successful it must be planned. Recognizing that the best-laid plans can go astray is an essential ingredient of life itself. Taking on the responsibility of planning your own career does expose you to the dangers involved, but they are in reality no greater than the dangers of not doing it. By expecting your employer to take care of your career you are simply saying 'If I don't get promotion or if my job is made redundant it's not *my* fault'. The choice is a clear one – make the journey or stay at home. It is the choice between maintaining the status quo with the certainty that *nothing* will happen to you or taking on the responsibility of making the journey knowing that, in all probability, *good things* will happen.

For many of us, it is not so much fear of travelling that concerns us but fear of *arriving*. As the saying goes 'I'm not afraid of flying – just terrified of crashing'. So it is not specifically risk itself that scares us but *failure*, or more accurately, *observable failure*. Personal career failure is not always visible to others unless it ends in redundancy and then it is *very* visible. The Career Menopause and failure to win that promotion is invisible to all but those who know or care about such things – that is why we may not find it too uncomfortable to stay in a job after our career has effectively ceased. Indeed, as we have seen 'job security' is in itself a sign of success to many people.

Personal career management *is* visible to others and does require the character to be seen to make mistakes *but not feel bad about it*. A failed objective is no more than that – a failed objective. It does not make *you* a failure. People are afraid to apply for jobs for two reasons: fear of rejection and fear of success.

*Fear of rejection*
No one enjoys being turned down, whether applying for a job or membership of a club or asking someone for a date. *Inaction* is of course guaranteed to avoid rejection and hence remove the fear. It is hardly surprising that we take rejection so personally, but this doesn't really stand up to close examination. Failure to achieve a job interview is not *personal* rejection because at this point they haven't seen you – they are only rejecting your *sales literature*. Failure to secure a job offer after an interview doesn't mean that you couldn't have done the

job – it means that somebody else did a better job of convincing them that *they* could. The degree of personal failure you should feel is dependent upon whether the failure was a result of factors within your control or *outside* your control – of which there are many. Whatever the reason, these 'failures' are no more than failed objectives along a path that must ultimately end in success.

### Fear of success

Strange as it might seem, achieving a job offer very often imbues us with a sense of fear. A new job is invariably a daunting prospect and self-doubt can creep in: 'Can I *really* do it? Am *I really* as good as I said I was?' Such fear is more often than not quite irrational, yet it can and does stop us from applying for jobs and encourages us to turn down interviews. Inertia can set in because the temptation to 'stick with what we know' is insuperable.

## Get the action habit

Inertia is the tendency of a body to preserve its state of rest unless acted upon by an external force. In the context of career management there are only two external forces that can be applied: promotion/job change or redundancy. If neither of these forces is being applied your career is not necessarily inert – promotion *now* may be unlikely or inappropriate for many understandable reasons which ought not to give cause for alarm.

It really comes down to the use of time, a precious and finite commodity. It certainly should give you cause for concern if you have been in your present position long enough to have learnt all the necessary skills, given the job your personal imprint and bypassed the date by which you could reasonably have expected some form of career development. In such a circumstance the force to move your career forward must come from within, ie yourself.

Many employers view with suspicion anyone who has been

in the same job for more than three years – they see it as a sign of career inertia/lack of ambition. Here we come to a point so fundamental it should be displayed in neon lights. It is the second law of personal career management:

*The longer you preserve your state of rest the less attractive you become to other employers.*

If your career is in this inert state, you are marking time and adding nothing to your CV. You simply must assume control of your own career: the only way to effect change is through action. It is action that makes things *happen*. Become a *pro*-active career manager rather than a *re*active employee. Pro-active people go forward, reactive people stay where they are, or even go backwards. To go forward you must have the capacity for *seeing* forward. You may be vegetating at the moment but don't dwell on your situation as it is – be positive and try to see it as it is going to be in the future.

The initial actions you take need not be hugely significant. Set *time* aside to work on your personal career plan. You can make a useful start by blowing the dust off your CV and bringing it up to date. You can indulge in the luxury of some self-analysis, identify your needs and any constraints that might militate against achieving them. Write down the possible options (Part 2 will help you here). Look for reasons why your objectives should and could be attained and resist the temptation to put actions into the 'too difficult' category. List any of your skills which are transferable and might be seen as an asset by other employers or in other fields. Research your potential market.

The list of initial actions you can make is almost limitless and at this stage none of them commit you to making an irrevocable decision about leaving your present employer. Indeed, the very action of constructing your CV may well lead you to conclude that your career is not stagnating as much as you thought. But it should give you a clue to when it *will* begin to stagnate, for which you can make your contingency plans – you are now employing *vision*.

Develop a plan and set targets. At some stage in the process it might be advisable to indicate discreetly to your present employer that you are making positive moves towards broadening your career outside the company. Action really does speak louder than words and will always provoke a *reaction*. Leaving them in no doubt that you are of serious intent and mean business may jolt them out of any complacency *they* have been showing – it really is amazing how much more attractive you can become when you are on the verge of breaking camp. If, however, they really can't offer you something better then clearly you were correct in thinking about moving on.

Remember that applying for other jobs and receiving offers does not commit you to accepting them. Just as employers will advertise mythical jobs purely as an exercise in assessing the state of the market, with no intention of recruiting anyone, so you can apply for jobs that you may not accept if offered.

---

**Action checklist**

■ Question your *motives* for staying where you are
■ Up-date your CV
■ Explore the alternatives

---

# CHAPTER THREE

## *Breaking Out*

### *Look before you leap*

### How visible are you?

Before seeking career progression with another employer be certain that opportunities with your current employer are as remote as they appear. Assuming that lack of ability or ambition is not holding you back, and that your employer has needs that you could fulfil, it may be that you are not *projecting* your attributes strongly enough. Ask yourself honestly, how hard do you push your claims for either promotion or a job change which would allow you to develop new skills? There is more to it than simply letting people know that you want to progress. Do you *indicate* that you have what it takes?. The personal qualities needed to progress 'in house' are exactly those required to achieve a better position outside. You must do a self-marketing job so that you and your talents become *visible* to those who are in a position to influence your future.

If you are a shrinking violet the fact that you achieve excellent results for your employer will be irrelevant – in fact it may encourage them to keep you where you are. Perhaps understandably, some employers are reluctant to change a winning formula, and if your immediate superiors are pleased with your work it is in their personal interest to adopt an 'if it ain't broke don't fix it' policy.

This, of course, is one of the great ironies of personal career management – department heads are invariably desperate to keep hold of good staff, even if it means stopping their progress. Alternatively, they are just as anxious to lose bad staff and if promoting them is the only way to do it, they may resort to it. The world of employment is full of unsung heroes who regard personal 'trumpet-blowing' as somehow demeaning. But to progress you must be prepared to bang on a few doors – not only must you be able to do the business, you must ensure that you are *seen* to be doing it. Just as excessive humility is the curse of the job-seeker it can be a very real barrier to personal career progress, which brings us to the third law of personal career management:

*Opportunities will often be denied to those whom it is believed will display the least offence at being overlooked.*

Broadening your career within your present organization demands that you take credit for your achievements and don't allow others to steal your thunder. Physical isolation from the decision-making machinery can be a problem, as can a personality clash with your immediate superior. But these can both be overcome if you are able to identify the people most likely to promote your cause and then proceed to cultivate them. Such people need not be senior people in the department you wish to leave; they are more likely to be those in positions of influence within that part of the organization you would like to join.

Learn from those already in the position to which you aspire. How well do they achieve results? What are their strengths and weaknesses? How would you do the job differently/better? How do they relate to others within the organization? Do they have a strong reputation? Why? Observing others in this way will nearly always boost your confidence. Human nature will dictate that you concentrate upon their weaknesses, but identifying their strengths will also provide you with the evidence to show that there is nothing superhuman about them.

Success really is a combination of ability and ambition. In many cases an abundance of the latter can compensate for any lack of the former – but the reverse rarely applies, for very few have greatness thrust upon them. It must be both sought and fought for. However distasteful an element of *conceit* may seem, it is a vital component of career progress.

Personal visibility tends to diminish in inverse proportion

to the size of your organization: the larger the organization the harder you will have to work to ensure a high profile. However, the smaller the organization the fewer opportunities there may be for you to progress, despite enhanced visibility. This is an important consideration when deciding whether to stay or leave.

Take a critical look at your achievements in your present position. If, for example, you have made innovations which have increased efficiency and perhaps lowered costs, are *they* aware of it? If not it can only be that you have failed to *make them* aware of it.

Often we become blasé about our achievements and simply see them as part of the job, but others are likely to see them as more significant. Clocking up 'brownie points' has traditionally been the object of mirth and derision by colleagues in the workplace – but invariably such people themselves have much to be modest about.

---

**Action checklist**

■ Ensure maximum visibility within your organization
■ Cultivate those in positions of influence
■ Learn from those in positions to which you aspire
■ Identify your priorities

---

## *Self analysis*

### Which priority?
The prospect of impending change presents you with an opportunity to examine your priorities in terms of *your* needs. If you are not doing what you want to do, are not where you want to be and are not receiving decent remuneration, then there must be room for improvement.

Money, job satisfaction and an ideal location are by no means incompatible but it is a rare bird indeed who is fortunate enough to hit the jackpot and secure all three. Some people do have satisfying work at a good salary and in a pleasant location. Others put up with a pittance for doing an unrewarding job in uncongenial surroundings. Most of us probably fall somewhere between the two extremes and, realistically, compromise is the order of the day. Any search for new employment should therefore be directed by a clear understanding of what your priorities are, because only then can you at least try to ensure that you will not end up compromising on your number one priority.

If money is your priority, and you have until now been an *employee*, then it is very likely that if you continue to work for someone else you will always be financially frustrated. You have probably been too busy earning a living to make any money and it is worth remembering that it is the employer who *makes* the money while the employee *earns* it. Perhaps you should give more serious thought to self-employment than you have in the past? Too many of us dismiss such a thought too quickly and hastily place self-employment in the 'too difficult' category, but self-employment is very much like job-hunting – if you go about it professionally and with self-discipline the risks will be minimized and success will come. There is no lack of advice and support for the budding entrepreneur.

Is your main priority *where* you live and work rather than salary of job satisfaction? The ideal location for yourself and your family can indeed compensate for a poorly paid and less satisfying job. The degree of difficulty in achieving this priority will depend upon a number of factors – not least upon personal finances and prevailing housing and employment opportunities. The good news is that in more rural areas property prices and the cost of some consumer items tend to be appreciably lower than in more densely populated parts of the country. However, job opportunities in these areas are fewer and such jobs as there are tend to be less remunerative.

Job-hunting within a strictly defined geographical area can be less difficult than following a 'go anywhere' philosophy.

Job-seekers for whom location is important but who, through panic or poor planning, apply for jobs all over the place are in serious danger of ending up where they don't want to be. So start by defining your desired location and establishing the maximum distance you are prepared to travel to work.

As we have seen in previous chapters, lack of job satisfaction is a classic symptom of the Career Menopause. Though important to most of us, it can be very elusive – for many that 'Monday morning feeling' is a daily occurrence. The reasons for this can be many and varied but some degree of re-training may well help.

As an employee you will have to work extremely hard and have a certain amount of good fortune to maximize your chances of achieving all three of the above objectives. (If you do find that you have to compromise, however, be sure to avoid compromising on that which is most important to you and your family.) Achieving all three is by no means impossible and if you have identified your main priority then the other two may well fall into place.

If you choose to be your own boss, it is far more likely that all three objectives will be met. Self-employment is not necessarily a panacea for career inertia and it will only work if you have something to sell that others wish to buy, but those for whom self-employment has been a success will probably testify that they have set up their business where they want to be, are receiving financial benefits and that job satisfaction has never been greater.

## Narrowing the search

If you are seeking a job within your specialization it should not be too difficult to identify *what* you are selling and match this to potential job opportunities. If, however, you are considering changing your career entirely or persuing the option of self-employment then a major self analysis is required to help you realize your abilities, preferences and limitations, and match them to career options.

Self analysis is really no more than seeking answers to the following six questions:

- What is my experience?
- What skills has this given me?
- What achievements have I as evidence of these skills?
- Which skills do I enjoy using and want to carry on using?
- Are there any gaps in my skills or knowledge which will diminish my chances of getting the right job?
- Who, in my chosen geographical area, might want to buy these skills?

The answers to the first three questions can be found by looking closely at the jobs you have done in the past, since our skills develop out of the experiences we have. In turn, *achievements* are what we get as a result of utilizing our skills, and they are the *evidence* we can present to potential employers.

Effective skill statements have two elements: skill and experience. Examples of each are as follows:

| *Skill* | *Experience* |
|---------|--------------|
| Advising | sales reps on quotas/targets |
| Demonstrating | new products to retailers |
| Distributing | sales literature to customers |

More effective skill statements have three elements: skill, experience and achievement. For example:

| *Skill* | *Experience* | *Achievement* |
|---------|--------------|---------------|
| Motivating | UK sales force | to increase sales |

Even more effective skill statements consist of the three elements plus *quantification* of achievement. For example:

| *Skill* | *Experience* | *Achievement/Quantification* |
|---------|-------------|------------------------------|
| Motivating | UK sales force | to increase sales by 30 per cent pa. |

The *very* best skill statements consist of three elements plus quantification and *intrigue*. For example:

| *Skill* | *Intrigue* | *Experience* | *Achievement/Quantification* |
|---------|-----------|-------------|------------------------------|
| Devising | unique | incentive scheme | to increase profits by £100,000 in first year |

Experience generally falls into one or more of the following categories: Verbal, Analytical, Organizational, Demonstrational, Managerial and Creative. These can be more easily understood as follows:

| Verbal | ⟶ | Talked to |
|--------|---|-----------|
| Analytical | ⟶ | Found out |
| Organizational | ⟶ | Sorted out |
| Demonstrational | ⟶ | Showed how |
| Managerial | ⟶ | Set up/In charge of |
| Creative | ⟶ | Made better |

Each of the following skill statement development exercises is headed by one of the above descriptions of an experience, eg 'Talked to'. In the left hand column Who/what? write down *who* you talk(ed) to during the course of your work. Write this down next to the Skill description word in the centre column which describes most accurately the function you are/were performing. In the right hand column To achieve what? write down what you achieved as a result. For example:

**Verbal experience**
|
**Talked to**
|

| Who/What? | Skill description | To achieve what? |
|---|---|---|
| Sales reps | Advising | On results of |
| | Addressing | market research |
| | Controlling | |
| Customers/Retailers | Demonstrating | New products |
| | Directing | |
| | Guiding | |
| | Instructing | |
| Public | Interviewing | Identify customer |
| | Leading | needs |
| | Liaising | |

The above example produces the following skill statements:

- Advising sales force on market research analysis
- Demonstrating new products to consumers/ retailers
- Interviewing the public to identify consumer needs

Now, using this technique go through each exercise and fashion *as many skill statements as you can*. (Don't worry about repetition – some skills will inevitably overlap with others.)

**Verbal experience**
↓
**Talked to**
↓

| Who/What? | Skill description | To achieve what? |
|---|---|---|
| | Addressing | |
| | Advising | |
| | Controlling | |
| | Co-ordinating | |
| | Counselling | |
| | Demonstrating | |
| | Directing | |
| | Encouraging | |
| | Guiding | |
| | Instructing | |
| | Interviewing | |
| | Leading | |
| | Liaising | |
| | Marketing | |
| | Mediating | |
| | Motivating | |
| | Negotiating | |
| | Ordering | |
| | Performing | |
| | Presenting | |
| | Promoting | |
| | Proposing | |
| | Providing | |
| | Recommending | |
| | Recruiting | |
| | Representing | |
| | Resolving | |
| | Selling | |
| | Teaching | |
| | Training | |
| | Translating | |

**Analytical experience**
|
**Found out**
|

| Who/What? | Skill description | To achieve what? |
|---|---|---|
| | Analyzing | |
| | Assessing | |
| | Classifying | |
| | Collating | |
| | Defining | |
| | Designing | |
| | Devising | |
| | Establishing | |
| | Evaluating | |
| | Forecasting | |
| | Identifying | |
| | Interpreting | |
| | Interviewing | |
| | Investigating | |
| | Researching | |
| | Testing | |
| | Tracing | |
| | Verifying | |

**Organizational experience**

**Sorted out**

| Who/What? | Skill description | To achieve what? |
|---|---|---|
| | Arranging | |
| | Assessing | |
| | Budgeting | |
| | Classifying | |
| | Collating | |
| | Composing | |
| | Conceiving | |
| | Conducting | |
| | Controlling | |
| | Co-ordinating | |
| | Decreasing | |
| | Defining | |
| | Distributing | |
| | Editing | |
| | Eliminating | |
| | Establishing | |
| | Evaluating | |
| | Identifying | |
| | Improving | |
| | Investigating | |
| | Itemizing | |
| | Modernizing | |
| | Operating | |
| | Organizing | |
| | Planning | |
| | Preparing | |
| | Processing | |
| | Producing | |
| | Redesigning | |
| | Reducing | |
| | Refining | |

**Organizational experience**
|
**Sorted out**
|

| Who/What? | Skill description | To achieve what? |
|-----------|-------------------|------------------|
|           | Reorganizing      |                  |
|           | Researching       |                  |
|           | Resolving         |                  |
|           | Reviewing         |                  |
|           | Revising          |                  |
|           | Scheduling        |                  |
|           | Simplifying       |                  |
|           | Solving           |                  |
|           | Streamlining      |                  |
|           | Transforming      |                  |
|           | Uncovering        |                  |
|           | Verifying         |                  |
|           | Vetting           |                  |

**Demonstrational experience**
|
**Showed how**
|

| Who/What? | Skill description | To achieve what? |
|---|---|---|
| | Advising | |
| | Coaching | |
| | Conducting | |
| | Demonstrating | |
| | Directing | |
| | Guiding | |
| | Illustrating | |
| | Instructing | |
| | Leading | |
| | Performing | |
| | Presenting | |
| | Teaching | |
| | Training | |

**Managerial experience**
|
**Set up/In charge of**
|

| Who/What? | Skill description | To achieve what? |
|---|---|---|
| | Administering | |
| | Approving | |
| | Composing | |
| | Conceiving | |
| | Conducting | |
| | Controlling | |
| | Co-ordinating | |
| | Creating | |
| | Designing | |
| | Developing | |
| | Devising | |
| | Directing | |
| | Establishing | |
| | Founding | |
| | Generating | |
| | Heading | |
| | Implementing | |
| | Initiating | |
| | Instituting | |
| | Introducing | |
| | Inventing | |
| | Launching | |
| | Leading | |
| | Managing | |
| | Opening | |
| | Originating | |
| | Pioneering | |
| | Planning | |
| | Preparing | |

**Managerial experience**
↓
**Set up/In charge of**
↓

**Who/What?**     **Skill description**     **To achieve what?**
Producing
Promoting
Representing
Starting

**Creative experience**

**Made better**

| Who/What? | Skill description | To achieve what? |
|---|---|---|
| | Broadening | |
| | Building | |
| | Combining | |
| | Consolidating | |
| | Constructing | |
| | Converting | |
| | Cutting | |
| | Decreasing | |
| | Developing | |
| | Devising | |
| | Doubling | |
| | Editing | |
| | Eliminating | |
| | Expanding | |
| | Improving | |
| | Increasing | |
| | Innovating | |
| | Minimizing | |
| | Modernizing | |
| | Redesigning | |
| | Reducing | |
| | Refining | |
| | Reorganizing | |
| | Resolving | |
| | Restructuring | |
| | Revising | |
| | Saving | |
| | Servicing | |
| | Simplifying | |
| | Solving | |
| | Streamlining | |

**Creative experience**
|
**Made better**
|

| Who/What? | Skill description | To achieve what? |
|---|---|---|
| | Strengthening | |
| | Transforming | |
| | Trimming | |
| | Uncovering | |
| | Unifying | |
| | Widening | |

Having completed the above exercise for each of your previous jobs, you will now have a list of skill statements which incorporates skills, experience and achievements. Now do the exercise again but this time analyzing the experiences you have had *outside* the workplace. Typically this will cover social, sporting, cultural or other voluntary pursuits. It is very important that you do this because:

1. **It will identify skills which are *transferable* and which correlate to those skills you have already identified**. This will provide additional evidence to place before potential employers.

2. **It will help to answer our third question, 'Which skills do I enjoy using and want to carry on using?'** We have already established that we are most likely to be good at the things we enjoy doing, so this part of the exercise can be an even more accurate pointer towards your future.

Now go back to your list and separate those that you did *not* enjoy from those that you did. Do not throw away your list of 'unenjoyable' skill statements – you will need them later.

Be honest and objective. Your opinion must be based upon your best recollection of how you felt *at the time*. The passage of time encourages us to deposit the good bits in our memory and consign the remainder to some permanently sealed dustbin at the back of our minds. Self analysis means taking the lid off this and having a peek.

First, let's deal with your list of 'enjoyable' skill statements which, although they have been culled from the past, have now been taken out of their historical context. The objective now is to prioritize the skills by asking yourself *why* each was so enjoyable. What was it that made it so rewarding? Identify the *motivators*. There is of course no one set of motivators which apply equally to all of us, but some examples of motivators (to which we all respond differently) are:

- Responsibility for things
- Responsibility for people
- Opportunities for advancement
- Congenial 'atmosphere'
- Status
- Authority
- Salary
- Interesting/challenging work
- Security
- Sense of achievement
- Recognition from others
- Teamwork
- Working alone
- Setting goals
- Meeting deadlines set by others
- Pressure
- Geographical location
- Small organization
- Large organization
- Repetitive work
- Variety
- Danger/insecurity

The above list is not exhaustive. If you can identify other motivators that work for you then add them to the list.

You now have two lists – skills and motivators. Number each skill and award a letter to each motivator. In the matrix on page 45 the skills are represented vertically in the left hand column, the motivators are represented horizontally along the top. For each of your skill statements identify which motivator allowed you to *enjoy* that experience. If more than one motivator was present then tick each box accordingly.

Once you have completed this exercise for each skill, add up the number of ticks in each vertical column. Write the total number in the box at the bottom of each vertical column. This will tell you the relative frequency of certain motivators – the more times a motivator appears the more important it is to you. To prioritize your skills add up the number of ticks in each horizontal column. Write the total number in the box on the right. **Note:** You may well have used a skill on more than one occasion, in which case either number it separately or tick the appropriate box more than once.

Along the horizontal columns the frequency of different motivators for each skill is an indicator of the importance of that skill to you.

At the end of the exercise place both skills and motivators in priority order, for example:

| Key | Skills | No. of motivators |
|---|---|---|
| 14 | Presenting information verbally to large groups | 11 |
| 7 | Planning cost-effective routes for product distribution | 9 |
| 8 | Liaising closely with Main Board Directors | 7 |
| 9 | Analyzing results of market research to maximize sales | 6 |
| 13 | Assessing effectiveness of product-promotion initiatives | 5 |

| Skills | Motivators | | | | | | | | | | | | | | | | | | | | | | | | | | Total |
|---|---|---|---|---|---|---|---|---|---|---|---|---|---|---|---|---|---|---|---|---|---|---|---|---|---|---|---|
| | A | B | C | D | E | F | G | H | I | J | K | L | M | N | O | P | Q | R | S | T | U | V | W | X | Y | Z | |
| 1 | | | | | | | | | | | | | | | | | | | | | | | | | | | | |
| 2 | | | | | | | | | | | | | | | | | | | | | | | | | | | | |
| 3 | | | | | | | | | | | | | | | | | | | | | | | | | | | | |
| 4 | | | | | | | | | | | | | | | | | | | | | | | | | | | | |
| 5 | | | | | | | | | | | | | | | | | | | | | | | | | | | | |
| 6 | | | | | | | | | | | | | | | | | | | | | | | | | | | | |
| 7 | | | | | | | | | | | | | | | | | | | | | | | | | | | | |
| 8 | | | | | | | | | | | | | | | | | | | | | | | | | | | | |
| 9 | | | | | | | | | | | | | | | | | | | | | | | | | | | | |
| 10 | | | | | | | | | | | | | | | | | | | | | | | | | | | | |
| 11 | | | | | | | | | | | | | | | | | | | | | | | | | | | | |
| 12 | | | | | | | | | | | | | | | | | | | | | | | | | | | | |
| 13 | | | | | | | | | | | | | | | | | | | | | | | | | | | | |
| 14 | | | | | | | | | | | | | | | | | | | | | | | | | | | | |
| 15 | | | | | | | | | | | | | | | | | | | | | | | | | | | | |
| 16 | | | | | | | | | | | | | | | | | | | | | | | | | | | | |
| 17 | | | | | | | | | | | | | | | | | | | | | | | | | | | | |
| 18 | | | | | | | | | | | | | | | | | | | | | | | | | | | | |
| 19 | | | | | | | | | | | | | | | | | | | | | | | | | | | | |
| 20 | | | | | | | | | | | | | | | | | | | | | | | | | | | | |
| 21 | | | | | | | | | | | | | | | | | | | | | | | | | | | | |
| 22 | | | | | | | | | | | | | | | | | | | | | | | | | | | | |
| 23 | | | | | | | | | | | | | | | | | | | | | | | | | | | | |
| 24 | | | | | | | | | | | | | | | | | | | | | | | | | | | | |
| 25 | | | | | | | | | | | | | | | | | | | | | | | | | | | | |
| 26 | | | | | | | | | | | | | | | | | | | | | | | | | | | | |
| 27 | | | | | | | | | | | | | | | | | | | | | | | | | | | | |
| 28 | | | | | | | | | | | | | | | | | | | | | | | | | | | | |
| 29 | | | | | | | | | | | | | | | | | | | | | | | | | | | | |
| 30 | | | | | | | | | | | | | | | | | | | | | | | | | | | | |
| 31 | | | | | | | | | | | | | | | | | | | | | | | | | | | | |
| 32 | | | | | | | | | | | | | | | | | | | | | | | | | | | | |
| 33 | | | | | | | | | | | | | | | | | | | | | | | | | | | | |
| 34 | | | | | | | | | | | | | | | | | | | | | | | | | | | | |
| 35 | | | | | | | | | | | | | | | | | | | | | | | | | | | | |
| 36 | | | | | | | | | | | | | | | | | | | | | | | | | | | | |
| 37 | | | | | | | | | | | | | | | | | | | | | | | | | | | | |
| 38 | | | | | | | | | | | | | | | | | | | | | | | | | | | | |
| 39 | | | | | | | | | | | | | | | | | | | | | | | | | | | | |
| Total | | | | | | | | | | | | | | | | | | | | | | | | | | | | |

| *Key* | *Motivators* | *Frequency* |
|---|---|---|
| D | Setting goals | 12 |
| B | Status | 11 |
| Q | Recognition from others | 10 |
| L | Large organization | 7 |
| A | Authority | 6 |
| G | Salary | 5 |

Providing you have gone about this exercise diligently and not cut corners, the resulting information will be of vital importance to you on at least three occasions:

1. **In Part 2 we will be looking at the possible options open to you.** Certain options require particular skills and motivators. These may well be in accord with those you have identified for yourself – if not, then taking that option may be unwise.

2. **In Part 3 we will be analyzing the job search – an option which for many of you will be the *only* option.** In this exercise we have already begun to identify what you are selling to potential employers. Much of this information will need to be set out on your CV.

3. **As we shall discover in Part 3, achieving a job offer is only part of the battle.** Assessing the quality of the offer is an art in itself. An obvious means of doing this is to establish whether the job will allow you to use the skills you enjoy *and* provide you with the necessary motivators.

You have now found the answers to four of the six questions posed on page 31. Question five 'Are there any gaps in my skills or knowledge which will diminish my chances of getting the right job?' will be dealt with in Part 2 Chapter Six. Question six 'Who, in my chosen geographical area, might want to buy these skills?' will be discussed in Part 3 Chapter Eight.

## A cautionary note

Throughout Part 1 we have looked at the Career Menopause and paid particular attention to the reasons why we have an alarming tendency to hold on to the wrong job. Inertia, fear, 'loyalty', 'security', complacency and our natural resistance to change are all factors which dissuade us from seeking greener pastures. Hopefully you may now have found the key (or keys) which has kept you locked in to the wrong job.

If so, you now have a choice: you can continue to let 'them' manage your career or you can *take control*. If the music is beginning to stop then things are likely to be happening around you which are causing you to *react*. Although you are the captain of your personal ship of progress you have let others take the helm. This is fine as long as the ship is taking you to where you want to be but a sudden change of direction means you must either stay for an unfulfilling trip or take the helm and steer a new course.

If you have chosen to take control it is essential to understand now that personal career management, like recruitment, is not an exact science. A change of employer may well be appropriate but there is little point in moving from one wrong job to another. What factors do you need to consider to ensure that this will not happen? Unfortunately there is no set formula to prevent this, but there are two basic questions to ask before accepting an offer from a new employer:

1. **Does the job allow me to broaden my career?** If it does not provide some kind of progression it might be unwise of you to accept it. Real career development is all about getting a better job than the one you already have, and a better job is always one which gives you the opportunity to develop *new* skills or consolidate those skills you already have by taking on *new* responsibilities.

2. **Is the financial package an improvement upon my present remuneration?** If it is not then think very carefully before accepting it, even if the job itself will allow you to broaden your career. The only exception to this might be if you were really changing career direction and moving from relatively highly paid employment to traditionally lower paid employment, eg from high technology to social work.

A new job which adds nothing to your career progression can be very difficult to explain away at subsequent job interviews. The reasons for your moving from XYZ to ABC will be of great interest to employers and if the move presented you with no opportunity to add to your personal kitty of skills and responsibilities it will be difficult to justify. Lowering your salary can weaken your bargaining position when making the next move which, remember, may not be initiated by you.

The fourth law of personal career management is:

*Your next job will only last as long as your employer needs it.*

The fifth law of personal career management is:

*Your next move will be on your CV forever.*

---

**The five laws of personal career management**

■ Your CV is your passport to the future and you never know when you might be asked to travel, regardless of whether you want to go

■ The longer you preserve your state of rest the less attractive you become to other employers

■ Opportunities will often be denied to those whom it is believed will display the least offence at being overlooked

■ Your next job will only last as long as your employer needs it

■ Your next move will be on your CV forever

---

# Part Two

## *Exploring the Options*

# CHAPTER FOUR

## Working for Yourself

There are many books available which give excellent advice on how to start your own business – advice on the legal aspects, marketing, selling, pricing and other financial considerations. This is not the function of this Chapter. Our purpose here is to explore the 'why' as opposed to the 'how'. For many, making the decision is the most painful and important part of the whole process. Once it is made, the way will be clear for you to address the practical considerations.

The following pages are designed to assist you in reaching the *right* decision and as such raises many questions which, on first sight, may appear to be placing barriers at the entrance to the self-employment road. This is quite deliberate for the barriers are very real ones and not merely placed there as a disincentive.

To be successful, self-employment requires a specific blend of qualities, not all of which are possessed by those aiming to go down this road. As indicated in Part 1, self-employment can, and has been, the right vehicle through which many have achieved their objectives. For others it has been a journey of self-discovery, but one which has ultimately ended in financial and emotional disaster. If the content of the next few pages is in itself enough to turn you away from this particular road then it will have done you a service.

### Understanding your motives
The transition from employee to self-employed is a huge step and demands a great deal of careful thought. We will see later that our capacity for self-delusion is almost infinite regarding the job search. Self-employment is no different. Your success in this field will depend upon many factors – not all of which will be under your control. The key to success is to effectively manage those factors which it *is* within your power to control.

One such factor is your ability to be objective about your rationale for 'going it alone'. If you are seriously considering self-employment, it is likely that you already have a business idea or 'vehicle' through which this can be achieved. Alternatively, you may have a strong *desire* but are scratching your head for an idea. If you fall into the latter category your rationale may need to be put under the microscope. *Why* do you have the desire for self-employment? Do you really want to work for yourself? This question must be posed (and answered honestly) for it is essential that you take the self-employment road for *positive* reasons. To distinguish the difference between positive and negative reasons ask yourself if, by travelling down this road, your intention is to get somewhere or to *get away* from somewhere else.

Self-employment can of course take you away from certain things – eg the job search, the Career Menopause, employee status – but it has to be more than just an escape route. Typically, those between the ages of 35 and 55, when going through the Career Menopause (and particularly when thrown into the job market through redundancy) give much thought to the idea of self-employment – rightly so, as this can present them with an opportunity for it. However, their motivation largely derives from a belief that, at such an age, their chances of getting another job are slim or non-existent. (Part 3 explains why this need not be so.) Such negative motivation can also be a result of the bitterness and cynicism one can feel when going through the trauma of redundancy – one way of ensuring that it cannot happen again is to work for oneself. Although these negative motivators are understandable it is arguable whether they are in themselves a sound basis for going it alone.

It is possible of course that you have both positive *and* negative reasons for considering self-employment. This can make the issue more complicated but if you have suddenly become unemployed it might be worth asking yourself 'If I had not become involuntarily unemployed would I have just carried on working for someone else or might I have "taken the plunge" and left to set up on my own?' If your answer is 'I believe I would have left anyway to develop my business idea' then your motivation is probably sound. If your response is to say 'No, if I still had my job I would have no incentive to go it alone' then you need to think things through far more carefully.

## Do you have what it takes?

Unfortunately, there is no established formula for deciding whether you are suitable for self-employment. Personal suitability is just as important as having a marketable business idea – one without the other is useless. So what *does* it take? Perhaps the fundamental difference between working for yourself and having a specific role as an employee is that with the former you need to be versatile enough to wear a number of different hats, often simultaneously.

### Functions you might have to perform if you were self-employed

- **Manager.** It will require you to possess the whole range of management skills, the most important of which is the self-discipline and motivation to *get things done*. As an employee you will have had a well-established routine, either devised by you or handed down from above. You will now have to establish a routine of your own and one which is geared to getting you to where you want to be ie running a successful business. Management has been defined as 'the ability to get results through other people'. As an employee you may have been a most effective manager and very able when it came to achieving results through others. Self-employment requires the same range of skills, regardless of whether you will be employing anyone else. The essential difference lies in the fact that the 'other people' upon whom your success is now dependent are those over whom you have *no direct authority* eg customers, clients, printers, distributors, suppliers – any one of a seemingly endless number of people can lose you credibility and money. As you will be entrusting others to perform certain tasks you will need to be an excellent judge of character and possess the 'inter-personal skills' to motivate them. It is also worth bearing in mind that such management will, more often than not, have to be performed over long distances and not 'from the office upstairs'.

- **Salesperson.** Your business will only succeed if you have something to sell that others wish to buy. One of the major causes of business failure is *inability to sell the product*. Even good products do not sell themselves – they must be brought to the attention of the market and this requires market analysis, identification of potential buyers and developing a strategy for getting the product in front of them. Selling a *service* is notoriously difficult, largely because there is rarely anything tangible to place in front of potential buyers – at least a product can be depicted in sales literature and/or be taken out of it's box, seen and held by the customer. A service has none of these benefits so your powers of imagination and persuasion need to be quite sophisticated. For every customer who will buy your product/service perhaps 100 won't. It takes persistence, belief, optimism, dedication and certainly a positive mental attitude to bounce back from continual rejection and make that sale. If you are sensitive, introspective, pessimistic and easily put off by failure you will not succeed.

- **Financial controller.** Controlling the finances of your business is the area where self-delusion tends to be greatest. It is all too easy to convince yourself that your business is doing better than it actually is. Such 'wishful thinking' can evolve from a variety of business errors:
a) Failure to take into account 'downtime' and overheads. For example, you may be charging what to you is a large fee for providing a service, eg consultancy, but does your pricing take into account any time spent on preparing or marketing? Will the fee provide you with enough income for those times when you will not be delivering the service?
b) Earnings projections based upon oral promises from customers that they will buy your product/service, but which they have not legally committed themselves to. In Part 3 we will see that you do not have a job until you receive the offer in writing: the same rule applies in business – oral promises don't pay the bills.

c) Cash-flow projections based upon products/services sold and delivered but not actually paid for. As with many small businesses, you may find that you have to expend more energy and devote more time to getting payment than it took to earn it.

d) Spending monies received from the business which should be set aside for other commitments eg VAT, Income Tax, National Insurance.

■ **Provider.** It is possible to get everything else right; the idea, selling the idea and pricing the idea but can you actually *deliver?* Once you are 'up and running' and have secured those first few vital sales can you satisfy the customer and *keep* the customer satisfied? The continued success of your business probably will depend greatly upon repeat business and *referrals.* This will only happen if customers feel that they are getting *value for money.* Quality control, after sales service and continual product/service development are all essential if you want to prevent customers from voting with their feet.

In the Self Analysis Exercise you identified those skills you enjoyed and the 'motivators' that were present. Go back to your lists and look again, particularly at the motivators. You placed your motivators in descending order of frequency. Your final list may have looked like this:

| *Motivators* | *Frequency* |
|---|---|
| Teamwork | 11 |
| Salary | 10 |
| Meeting deadlines set by others | 8 |
| Large organization | 8 |
| Security | 7 |
| Recognition from others | 6 |

*Or* it may have looked like this:

| *Motivators* | *Frequency* |
|---|---|
| Working alone | 11 |
| Pressure | 10 |

| | |
|---|---|
| Danger/insecurity | 8 |
| Variety | 8 |
| Setting goals | 7 |
| Sense of achievement | 6 |

If your list is very similar to the first example then consider *very* carefully the wisdom of going down the self-employment road. If it is more in tune with the second example you are probably a born entrepreneur. More realistically, your list of motivators may be a confusing mixture of both, but the frequency of certain motivators can be very useful when examining the self-employment option.

## Teamwork

Having this high on your motivator list does not necessarily make self-employment undesirable for you – you may be equally well disposed to working alone but have never had it put to the test. Self-employment will certainly do that. The majority of new entrepreneurs start off working alone and gradually build up a workforce. Many, however, have no intention of employing anyone else and plan to carry on being a 'one person band'. For them the isolation can be a merciful release from that constricting 'band of brothers' where perhaps they were obliged to proceed at the speed of the slowest member. For others the loneliness can prove to be unbearable and they find that the isolation severely limits their ability to function effectively. This factor alone can render a good business idea inoperable and you should give it serious consideration – the alternative is to find out the hard way.

## Salary

Again this is not necessarily a bad motivator to have on your list if you are considering self-employment. It depends very much on your interpretation and meaning of the term. If you mean 'I enjoy the benefits of a large and regular income' then self-employment is unlikely to be right for you. The first five years may well require you to lower your standard of living and forego all kinds of financial benefits enjoyed as someone else's employee, not least of which will be regular holidays. On the other hand, if you mean 'money is my motivating force and I continually strive to maximize my earning potential' then going into business may well be your forte. We saw in Part 1 that most businesses exist for one reason – to make profits. It really is quite surprising how many people go into business on their own account and yet espouse the idea that to them money isn't that important. Business and indifference to the profit imperative make strange bedfellows.

## Security

We saw in Part 1 that security in a job is largely a myth and no more than an excuse for inertia. The very nature of the 'security straitjacket' is such that the longer we are in it the riskier it becomes in terms of personal career development. As far as self-employment is concerned the reverse is true – the risk will diminish and security will be enhanced the longer you maintain your business on a profitable footing. This doesn't mean that you can become complacent – that is just as dangerous a pitfall when working for yourself as it is in a job. It does mean, however, that after five years or so of increasing success in your business it would require a severe lack of vision on your part or circumstances out of your control to cause it to fail. However, any *desire* for security, at least in the first few years, is not in itself a sound rationale for going it alone.

## Setting goals

This is an indispensable motivator and in direct contrast to 'meeting deadlines set by others'. The ability to set goals and achieve them is a sign of leadership which in turn is an essential component of management. You will need to be single-minded (and often bloody-minded), have the stamina to drive the business forward, be a 'can do' person and yet be flexible enough to change course in order to seize opportunities as and when they arise.

## Pressure

While some people do work better under pressure others simply collapse under the weight of it. Should you fall into the second category then begin an active job search without delay – self-employment is not a pleasant substitute for what to you may have been the pressurized environment of the workplace or indeed the job search itself. If you have always worked well under pressure, however, then this will stand you in good stead when going it alone.

Self-employment pressure can come in many diverse forms and from different directions. Pressure can occur in the form of *stress* and a most unexpected source of stress can be, not the business itself, but your own family. There is no point whatsoever in going into business on your own account if your family is not unreservedly enthusiastic about the prospect. You may thrive under pressure and enjoy 'living on the edge' but does your partner? You may be prepared to drop your standard of living but is your family?

If your family will be directly involved in the business, have you considered whether you can work together on what should be a more formal footing than you have been used to? Will you be working from home, and if so do you have the necessary facilities? Your partner may not be in full-time employment and perhaps has an established and effective routine for running the home. You will now be 'invading' that space and interfering with that routine while trying to impose one of your own. Do you have sufficient communications systems in place to cope with both business *and* family needs eg transport, telephone/answering machine, fax? The last thing you want is to become embroiled in a battle over family territorial rights. If your children are still at school will you be able to cope with the distractions when they are around during those long holidays? These may seem obvious points to make but many a budding entrepreneur has come unstuck through forgetting that the self-employment road, if taken, is rarely a journey taken alone.

---

**Do you have what it takes to become successfully self-employed?**

|  | YES | NO |
|---|---|---|
| ■ Positive motivation for self-employment | ☐ | ☐ |
| ■ Versatility/adaptability | ☐ | ☐ |
| ■ Self-discipline | ☐ | ☐ |
| ■ Self-motivation | ☐ | ☐ |
| ■ Excellent judgment of character | ☐ | ☐ |
| ■ People management skills | ☐ | ☐ |
| ■ Imagination | ☐ | ☐ |
| ■ Persuasion | ☐ | ☐ |
| ■ Persistence | ☐ | ☐ |
| ■ Optimism | ☐ | ☐ |
| ■ Dedication | ☐ | ☐ |
| ■ Positive mental attitude | ☐ | ☐ |
| ■ Objectivity | ☐ | ☐ |
| ■ Ability to deliver the product/service | ☐ | ☐ |
| ■ Ability to work alone | ☐ | ☐ |
| ■ Profit-driven approach | ☐ | ☐ |
| ■ Vision | ☐ | ☐ |
| ■ Willingness to take a calculated risk | ☐ | ☐ |
| ■ Ability to set goals | ☐ | ☐ |
| ■ Opportunism | ☐ | ☐ |
| ■ Ability to work well under pressure | ☐ | ☐ |
| ■ Supportive family | ☐ | ☐ |

---

## How sound is your idea?

Having established your personal suitability you can now go forward with confidence and put your idea to the test. This doesn't mean that you should make a decision to proceed and launch yourself along the road. It does mean that you undertake some kind of feasibility study in order to assess viability. Your idea may have been developed from your existing 'know how' or have arisen through your identifying a promising market. Of course know how and markets are both needed – if you have only one of these you will need to acquire the other.

Your idea need not be original. A sound idea with appropriate knowledge of markets and management can be successful even if it isn't new. At least it will have a track record of sorts, since it is probably a variation on an existing theme. It may have arisen through your seeing a product or service which appears to be commercially successful and identifying a market which could use it but in which it is not currently available, and now 'all' you have to do is introduce it to that market.

This is how self-employment can satisfy your priority in terms of geographical location – identify *where* you want to be and then establish what needs are not being satisfied there.

Whatever the source or nature of your business idea, to succeed it must satisfy a need. Furthermore, unless huge profits are going to be generated over a short period of time, that need must have an element of permanence, ie to provide a regular and ongoing income the need cannot be transitory and subject to the whims of trend or fashion. Also, if that need is already being satisfied by established competition then you must be able to offer a product/service which is better, different, less expensive or a combination of all three – in effect it has to be *competitive*.

## When need turns to desire

If you believe that you have identified a need you must ask yourself whether your potential customers are *aware* that they have a need. More often than not we don't know that we need something until someone tries to sell it to us. It is at this point that you might have to turn 'need' into *desire*. This is of course a matter of degree but, generally, the weaker the need the harder you will have to work to make the customer *want* whatever you are selling.

---

**Test the viability of your idea – and your ability to deliver it effectively to the market**

- Is the need already being satisfied, in part or in whole, by competitors?
- If so, what does your idea have ('unique selling points') that will give you the edge?
- Is the need permanent or transitory?
- Are potential customers aware that they need what you are selling?
- If not, *how* will you make them aware?
- Do they *really* need what you are selling or will their lives be largely unaffected by their failure to buy?
- If they can live without it how will you encourage them to desire it?

---

If you have already assessed yourself as being suitable for self-employment *and* you are able to come up with the right answers to the above questions then the chances are that you will succeed. At some point you will have to make a decision on whether or not to proceed, although if you are still in full-time employment it may be possible for you to develop your business plan – and even start your business in a small way – while still working. This can be a sensible way to avoid 'burning your boat' and committing yourself wholeheartedly to self-employment. At some point however you will still have to make a judgment on when to 'take off'.

---

**Hazard warning**

- If you choose the above option this may render you ineligible for the Government *Enterprise Allowance Scheme* which provides financial assistance and business advice to new business start-ups. Information on eligibility is available from Job Centres, and you should seek advice on the interpretation of 'starting your business' *before* proceeding.

---

If you are already unemployed then your dilemma may be more acute. In most cases it is not practicable to hedge your bets by attempting to proceed with your business idea *and* activate a meaningful job-search campaign. You will, in all probability, fall between two stools and fail to do justice to either.

Much prevarication at this point is a very strong indicator that you should take the job-search road. After all, you may now have the opportunity to go self-employed, your motives may be positive and your idea may be sound but *now* may not be the right time for market, financial or family reasons. Only you can decide.

## The price of failure

If you decide to take the self-employment route your mind will be focused on success and achieving your objectives. You will not therefore be entertaining any thoughts of failure – to do so at this point would be negative in the extreme and it would not auger well for the future. Yet, unpalatable as it might seem, now *is* the time to consider the implications of possible failure.

The personal, and financial 'downsides' of business failure should be self-evident, but whatever the cost in those terms your position will be such that the job-search road will provide your only realistic escape route. Should this scenario develop you may find that the road will be more narrow than it was before you became self-employed.

We have seen what it takes to start your own business: nerve, drive, commitment and enthusiasm, to name a few (and all qualities of interest to employers). We have also seen what it takes to be a success: planning, vision, management skills. If your business fails it is these skills that potential employers may have reason to question.

In addition, your *motives* for moving from employment to self-employment and back again may also come under the microscope. Here we return to the importance of understanding your motives. If you are trying to gain re-entrance to the

# The self-employment road

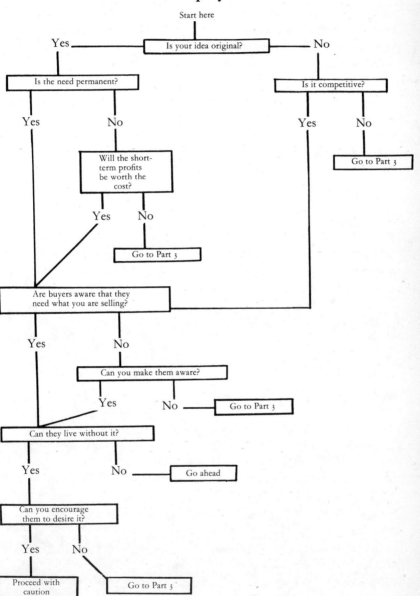

job market and your original reasons for leaving it were negative ones, employers will be entitled to ask what, if anything, has changed your feelings – apart from the fact that you are now in a bit of a hole.

This is not to say that you would never work again – that would be nonsense. It *is* to say that getting the right job may be that much more difficult from a position of failed self-employment, particularly if you interrupted a career that was professional/vocational in nature – your commitment to that career may now be questioned. Perverse as it might seem, in such a context does the career 'strait-jacket' become one that actually locks you *out*?

# CHAPTER FIVE

# *Franchising*

It has to be said that, if in the previous chapter you concluded that your motives for self-employment were 'impure' or that you really didn't have what it takes, then franchising is not for you either. If, however, your motives are sound and you do have what it takes, but simply lack the idea or vehicle through which you can make it happen then franchising could well provide the answer.

### *What is franchising?*

Franchising is a licence to trade under the franchisor's name (eg 'Wimpy', 'Body Shop') for a specified period of time and in a defined geographical area.

### *What are the benefits?*

The major benefit to the franchisee (ie *you*) could be described as one of risk minimization. The risks are reduced in the following ways:

- The business concept has already been tried, tested and found to work. However, even if the franchise operation is approved by the British Franchise Association (BFA) and adheres to it's Code of Practice there is no guarantee that it will be a success *for you*. That the concept has been a success for others (and in other areas) does not mean that you can take it 'off the shelf', set it up in your area and automatically expect it to flourish. You must research your market just as thoroughly as you would if starting your own business from scratch. Before committing yourself to franchising make contact with those who are already carrying out the same franchise operation in other areas – go along and talk to them, identify what problems they had to overcome and what degree of support they received from the franchisor

- The franchisor provides the entire business concept for the conduct of operations – in effect a complete business plan
- The franchisor provides back up and support services. This can be anything connected with the setting up of the business eg your training and the training of any staff, marketing assistance and help with financial/legal matters and planning applications
- The franchisor guarantees geographical protection, ie that none of its other franchisees will operate within your geographical area
- The clearing banks are more willing to offer loans for the setting up of recognized franchises than for new businesses
- The franchisor has a vested interest in the success of each franchise operation and is therefore unlikely to knowingly 'short change' its franchisees in terms of ongoing support

All things considered, then, it is small wonder that the majority of new franchises succeed whereas the majority of new businesses fail. Inevitably, and in the light of there being no such thing as a free lunch, there is a price to be paid. This takes the form of an initial investment fee plus a regular weekly or monthly royalty paid by the franchisee to the franchisor. The initial fee will vary considerably depending on the nature of the franchise: a 'fast food' operation with high capital investment and occupying a prime city centre site can cost in excess of £250,000; other franchises with low overheads and perhaps where the franchisee works from home can cost as little as £10,000.

One danger area regarding the ongoing royalty payments is that such payments are normally based on turnover and not profits. Problems can arise if turnover is large but profits remain small – this is obviously something to check out when talking to other franchisees, remembering of course that *their* turnover and profits will not necessarily be reflected in *yours*.

Ownership of the business is by the franchisee, who is free to sell the business on. However, the franchisor retains the right to approve both the sale and the incoming franchisee.

Compared to setting up your own business from scratch, franchising does appear to have quite solid and attractive advantages. The problems of franchising are more likely to arise from *success* than from *failure*. *Your* business can become a very personal thing and as it grows you may well find yourself adopting a very protective, possessive, even 'maternal', posture in respect of it (it's no coincidence that many people refer to their business as 'my baby'). With franchising there may come a point where you as the franchisee begin to resent your relationship with the franchisor. Much of the success will have been due to your efforts and it would not be unnatural to deny the benefits injected by the franchisor in those early days – with the passing of time you may develop an over-inflated view of your own input and importance.

Either way, it will be necessary, *before committing yourself to franchising*, to ask yourself whether you have got what it takes to enter into this kind of partnership and not subsequently resent it. Do you want and need complete autonomy? If so, forget franchising.

# CHAPTER SIX

## *P l u g g i n g   t h e*   **G** *a p s*

If self-employment is not for you then you might be forgiven for believing that your only remaining option is to find a permanent job. This may not necessarily be the case, at least not in the short term. Much will of course depend upon your personal situation and aims for the future. Indeed, if your aims are still confused then it may be advisable for you to buy yourself some time. But how can this be achieved and what are the advantages?

First, remember that you certainly want to avoid getting the *wrong* job. After completing the Self Analysis Exercise you will have a better understanding of your strengths/weaknesses and a clearer perception of what might constitute the *right* job. However, it is likely that this perception will be tinged with a feeling of uncertainty. Any misgivings may well be a direct result of your answer to our fifth question on page 31, 'Are there any gaps in my skills or knowledge which will diminish my chances of getting the right job?'

If your answer is yes then obviously such gaps must be identified and plugged. Gaps will normally fall into at least one of three categories:

1. **Experience**
2. **Skills**
3. **Academic**

The means of plugging these gaps are:

- Voluntary work
- Temporary work
- Further/higher education

## Voluntary work

Your initial reaction to the words 'voluntary work' may be to visualize yourself as some middle-class worthy dispensing tea and biscuits to the less fortunate. Yet, in theory, you can offer your services in a voluntary capacity to *anyone* – it is not necessary to join an established voluntary organization which traditionally provides a support service for the socially disadvantaged, though this would be an advisable option if your career ambitions lay in this area. Whether this is a realistic option for you will depend upon your financial position – you will have to forego a regular income for a period of time, though some voluntary organizations are in a position to pay certain expenses.

### The benefits of voluntary work

- **It is flexible.** If you are seeking to establish whether you have what it takes to do something different then identify who in your geographical area does that type of work and ask them if they would allow you to find the answer by working with them for free. Both parties benefit from such an arrangement. Most employers, if you approach them in the right way, should be amenable to such an arrangement – though you may encounter certain trade union objections.

- **It can plug *both* the skills and experience gaps,** though only if the employer is willing to give you 'hands on' experience as opposed to just being an observer or 'shadow'. However, even if the opportunities for this are limited, the arrangement will give you what might be described as 'environmental experience', ie an opportunity to assess if a particular type of working environment is a suitable one for you.

- **If you are unemployed (and particularly if, in addition, you live alone) it removes the trauma of isolation and gets you back into a working environment.** This in itself makes you privvy to the flow of information which, as we will see later, is food and drink to anyone seeking work. Isolation cuts off this flow.

■ **It provides excellent credentials for when you do start to apply for full-time paid employment.** To potential employers you will be sending both a message of intent and reassurance that you have what it takes.

■ **It can help you to find the right job.** Work experience, if closely related to what you perceive as being the *right* job, can provide you with further *hard evidence* on which to base your judgment.

■ **It can get you a job.** Performing well and displaying the necessary personal and professional qualities gives the organization you are with a great incentive to *create a job for you*. A period of voluntary 'no strings attached' work experience can remove any uncertainty the organization may have felt.

### *Temporary work*

This normally involves working directly for an agency which 'hires you out' to employing organizations on a long or short-term basis. The advantages of 'temping' are largely financial as you are earning an income while you decide on your next move, normally based on the number of hours worked.

By its very nature it is not a permanent commitment and, if described in the right way, will not look out of place on your CV. Although the fifth law of personal career management will still apply, the effect will not be damaging if your period of temping is linked in some way to jobs for which you will be subsequently applying. This can help to release some of the pressure of job-hunting and allow you to be more selective in your choice of a more permanent job. You will normally have control over the number of hours you work. This flexibility allows you to combine temping with the job search.

Apart from the above, temporary work does have most of the benefits outlined for voluntary work, but there is a distinct disadvantage – in the majority of cases the agency will be interested in you for your existing skills, for these will be what it is selling to its customers. The opportunity for you to plug the skills gap will therefore be limited – unless you can convince the agency that your skills are transferable to other environments.

### *Further/higher education*

This option, of course, plugs the academic gap. The lack of a professional or academic qualification is frequently a very real barrier to career progression, but in no way is this barrier insurmountable unless:

a) You lack the drive to do something about it, or
b) Your financial position is such that it is not a viable option.

This option raises many objections from those whose only way forward would be to take it. Do you feel that you 'couldn't go back to studying'? Of course you could! The chances are that you are more intellectually capable than earlier in your life. Remember, the whole purpose of the exercise is to go forward. If you view education negatively – ie as 'going back' – it can only be said that you have a somewhat antiquated notion that education necessarily begins at the age of five and ends in one's early twenties.

Do you feel that 'Three years in full-time education is a long time'? How long have you been in the wrong job – five years? Now *that's* a long time. Time itself is of little importance – it's what you *do* with your time that counts. How would you prefer to spend the next three years – studying for a qualification which will get you to where you want to be or toiling away at the wrong job? Consider also that your appropriate course of study may neither be three years in length nor full-time. The Open University, for example, provides a huge range of courses (not all degree courses) with a built-in flexibility which enables students to study at their own pace and in their own time. Eligibility for degree courses is on a 'first come first served' basis and there are no formal academic entrance requirements. In addition, it is even possible to begin an OU degree course and, at an appropriate point, transfer to a more conventional university to complete it.

Perhaps you think that 'At my age I'd feel out of place at a college or university'. No you wouldn't! Few people realize that 'mature students' already comprise a large proportion of the student population and are, on the whole, much sought after by educational establishments. Furthermore, this trend is likely to increase in the coming years in the light of diminishing numbers of school-leavers.

You don't always need 'A' levels. For mature students (which for most establishments usually means anyone over the age of 25) qualifications are not normally a pre-requisite for entrance. Applications are treated on their merits and the educational body will only be looking for *some evidence* of academic capability.

'I can't afford it' is another possible objection. You might be pleasantly surprised, however, when you look into it. If you haven't previously had a grant for a full-time course of study then the award of such a grant is mandatory. Grants for mature students are more generous than for others and are not linked to the income of parents.

Clearly, then, there are many reasons why the educational road can lead to success and few insurmountable reasons for not taking it. Quite apart from what you will get out of it in terms of qualifications, the experience itself can be rewarding in many ways and provide the perfect springboard from which to launch a second career.

# Part Three

# How to Find the Right Job

# CHAPTER SEVEN

# Doing the Groundwork

### The job-search

For most of us job-hunting is a rather hit and miss affair. Certainly, when dumped unceremoniously into the job market through redundancy we have an alarming tendency either to:

a) Run around like headless chickens and gratefully grab the first offer that comes our way, regardless of its suitability, *or*
b) Vegetate.

The good news is that from now on your competitors in the job market will carry on conducting such an amateurish search, while *you* will be actively pursuing a planned, methodical job-search *campaign*. As with most campaigns there is an enemy to be fought, and the enemy here is *time*. Time is money – if you had unlimited financial resources you probably wouldn't be looking for a job. The effective management of time is essential whether you are unemployed or seeking a better job while you still have one.

Job-hunting, although a serious business, is very much like a game and, as with all games, there are rules and tactics. There are also winners and losers, though, unfortunately, 'winning' and 'losing' actually has little to do with one's ability to do the job. Perfectly sound job applicants lose because they don't know how to play the game (or because they fail to realize that a game is on). They lose either through ignorance of the rules or because of their inability to put the rules into practice through innate lack of self-discipline, self-motivation and a positive mental attitude.

The eventual winner of the game is not necessarily the best person for the job. In fact, the vagaries of the job search are such that the best person for the job is frequently eliminated in the early stages. The one who wins the job offer, assuming there has been an element of fair competition, will always be the one who has *played the game the best*.

Knowing how to play the game is, then, the key to success. Part 3 will familiarize you with the rules and explain many of the tactics which have ensured success for thousands of job applicants. There is nothing 'mysterious' about it and much of what appears in this section is based upon logic, common sense and, more often than not, *courtesy* towards the people with whom you will be dealing. We will break down the job search into its various components, taking them one at a time and highlighting the multitude of hazards which have eliminated otherwise sound applicants.

### Understanding the job market
Not for nothing is it called the job *market*. You are entering a market like any other, except that here *you* are the product. However unedifying this thought may be, the whole process of recruitment and selection is conducted in much the same way as the buying and selling of consumer products.

Sometimes it is a buyers' (employers') market; sometimes, when the economy is strong, it is a sellers' (employees') market. Because the employer is the buyer the onus is on the seller to take the dominant role. Yet, traditionally, this has not been the case with this particular market. As job-hunters, we have become used to expecting the employer to make the running, and this has encouraged us to adopt a rather passive approach to the job search, resulting in the employer appearing to hold all the aces. It seems strange, also, that in no other market is the buyer *expected* to advertise a need. The job market should be no different – and as we shall see it *is* no different – from other markets.

To find the right job when you want it, and where you want it, requires a fundamental change in your attitude towards this relationship between buyer and seller. Employers have *needs* (and often quite urgent needs) that have to be fulfilled. You are potentially doing them a great favour by adopting the traditional role of seller, ie by making the first approach.

To understand the importance of this we need to take a closer look at the market. Research has shown that only about 25 per cent of available private sector jobs are ever advertised. Why? Because for many employers advertising is a *last resort*. It is time-consuming and thus expensive. It is also the least efficient way of filling jobs. To avoid encouraging hundreds of applicants, the buyer will often have to be more specific about experience, qualifications, age etc than is necessary. If the advertisement is not 'tightly' written the buyer will be swamped with applicants for whom the paperwork alone can tie down a personnel department (assuming there is one) for weeks. If they can get the right person through any other means *they will not hesitate to do so*. From your point of view responding to advertisements is unlikely to be particularly fruitful. (We will, however, take a closer look at this later on – ignoring a quarter of your market could be a dangerous tactic.)

How then are the other 75 per cent of vacancies filled? Let us take a quick overview of the market:

|  | % |
|---|---|
| Advertised | 25 |
| Agencies | 20 |
| Personal contact | 35 |
| Speculative | 20 |
|  | 100 |

*Advertised*
By this we mean any vacancy, or vacancies, publicized through media within the public domain – whether placed directly by the employer or through an agency.

*Agencies*
These are profit-making organizations acting as agents for the employer. Normally called 'search consultants' or, more colloquially, 'head-hunters', they will not advertise positions

but will either search for a specific person (normally in employment elsewhere) or 'trawl' through their existing data base of clients who have approached them speculatively.

*Personal contact*
Many people achieve job interviews/offers through developing a network of personal contacts including friends, neighbours, colleagues or business acquaintances.

*Speculative*
Some job interviews/offers are achieved by making direct 'applications' to targeted employers.

It is important to understand that not everyone shares the same job market. The following are factors which effect the market share.

## Age
The older you are the less likely it becomes that your job will be found through an advertisement. This is not because you couldn't do the job, nor even that they don't want you. More often than not it is simply a device used by the employer to 'tighten up' the advertisement and thus avoid having hundreds of applicants. The job market for a 55-year-old would probably look like this:

|  | % |
|---|---|
| Advertised | 10 |
| Agencies | 10 |
| Personal contact | 40 |
| Speculative | 40 |
|  | 100 |

Clearly, then, for anyone in this age category the emphasis must be on developing that personal network and making direct approaches. Happily, it is not unreasonable to suggest that the older you are the more personal contacts you will have built up over the years.

## Specialization

You will need to look carefully at your range of skills and identify the areas of employment in which they can be used. It may be that your skills are so highly specialized that only a handful of employers could use them. This is particularly so for those in the scientific field. The speculative approach should therefore form the main thrust of such a person's search. For example, anyone working in the computer/information technology field will be aiming at a different market. A high percentage of jobs in this area are found through agencies and the market is more likely to look like this:

|  | % |
| --- | --- |
| Advertised | 10 |
| Agencies | 70 |
| Personal contact | 10 |
| Speculative | 10 |
|  | 100 |

## Geographical

If your chosen geographical area lies within a rural or close-knit community then it is essential that you plug into the 'grapevine' which such areas typically develop. It is noticeable that in such areas advertised vacancies are few and far between. This is not necessarily because there are fewer jobs (although there often are) but because employers have no need to put themselves through the trauma of advertising – *they* will use the 'grapevine'. If this is your situation it is essential that you put the emphasis on developing personal contacts and making speculative approaches – these two routes are likely to account for a combined 80 per cent of your market.

Market sectors do of course overlap and the division is not always as clear as it would seem. Individuals within agencies are themselves personal contacts once you have opened up a line of communication – but, unlike other contacts, they do have many clients and are not motivated by altruism.

However, all contacts should be developed, and one of the rules of job-hunting is that once a line of communication has been opened it should be kept open. Similarly, a personal contact may not be in a position to arrange an interview for you but may pass on information which leads you to make a speculative approach. An advertisement may in itself be of no use regarding the job advertised, but the company advertising may be of sufficient interest to prompt you into making a speculative approach.

Your initial task is to identify as accurately as possible the breakdown of *your* market as you see it. Later on we will be looking more closely at how each of the four market sectors can be exploited by the alert job-seeker.

### Planning the campaign

As we have already established that time is the enemy then effective use of the time at your disposal is of paramount importance. You will run out of time when you run out of money: if your financial resources dwindle, turning down job offers because they are not 'right' for you will be a luxury you can't afford.

For the purpose of this section we will assume that you are seeking work from a position of unemployment and that you therefore have eight hours a day, five days a week at your disposal. From now on every day that goes by is costing you money.

### Setting the objective

Your objective is to find the best possible job in the shortest possible time. It is up to you to define what the 'right job' is – we all have different needs and priorities. If you are still in doubt, try looking again at the Self Analysis Exercise in Part 1. Your objective is to answer the final question posed on page 31: 'Who, in my chosen geographical area, might want to buy these skills?'

# How much time do I need?

When do you want to start your next job? 'As soon as possible' is an understandable reaction to the question but quite useless when it comes to planning the campaign. You must set a realistic target in terms of time.

For example, let's assume that your target is 1 July and that the job you want has been advertised and you have therefore been in competition with other applicants. If you are going to start the job on 1 July when will the employer need to offer it to you? (Hazard Warning: you do not have a job offer until you have it in writing – see page 178.) At executive level they are unlikely to offer you the job on 30 June and ask you to start the following day. They will normally expect that the successful applicant will have to give one month's notice and will have built this into *their* recruitment plan. Your target for receiving the job offer in writing, therefore, should be 3 June.

At executive level it is unusual to receive a job offer on the basis of one interview. In fact, for any 'white collar' job two interviews is the norm. At the second interview or 'shortlist' stage they might be seeing from two to six candidates. The successful candidate could expect to receive a written job offer around one week after the second interview. However, at this stage that candidate will begin to negotiate terms and conditions, will be having discussions with other 'buyers' and is just as likely to turn down the offer. If you are their second choice, therefore, you may not receive the written offer until three weeks after the second interview. So you should aim to attend your second interview by 13 May.

At the first interview stage, the buyer may be seeing up to a dozen candidates. This in itself is time-consuming, so you should allow one week for all the interviews to take place, one week for them to reach a decision on who to shortlist and another week for them to give reasonable notice regarding the second interview. This means that you should aim to attend your first interview by 22 April.

Unless the advertisement has been very 'tightly' written, or the job in question is very specialized, it will invite a huge response. It is by no means unusual for an advertised position to attract a hundred applications, and this makes it difficult to predict the time needed with any accuracy. It is not unknown for applicants to be called for a first interview *two months* after responding to the advertisement. The speed of the response will depend upon the number of applicants, the urgency of the buyer's need and its own efficiency, so all you can do is make a thoughtful guess at this stage. Let's say that you decide to allow three weeks to elapse between the date of application and the date of the first interview. You should therefore apply for a first interview by 1 April.

### *The above example gives us a number of quite fundamental rules:*

**1.** You will need to allocate *three months* to achieving your objective – or at least, you will need three months *minimum* if you are prepared to stick with the traditional method of searching for a job – solely responding to advertisements as and when they arise. The problem here is that the time factor is, to all intents and purposes, *out of your control* – you are only able to travel at the same speed as the buyer.

**2.** You cannot get a job without overcoming the hurdles of:
- achieving a first interview, and sometimes a second one
- achieving the job offer.

At any one of these stages you can *fail*. Unfortunately, it is likely that you will glide effortlessly over the first two hurdles only to receive a rejection on 3 June instead of a job offer. (This highlights the folly of adopting a 'linear' approach to the job search ie applying for one job at a time and then waiting to see if you overcome all the hurdles before applying for another. Rejection is certainly easier to cope with if you have other things happening to you.) Be prepared for rejection. You cannot and will not win them all. On no account take rejection personally. Remember that if you fail to achieve an interview it is not *you* they are rejecting (they haven't seen you!) but your sales literature. If you fail to achieve a second interview or a job offer it simply means that someone sold themselves better than you did.

**3.** Even if you get the job offer is it the *right* job offer? (Hazard Warning: turning down job offers can be difficult to justify to family and friends. To get around this let them know *beforehand* that you are going to be selective in your choice of job. If *they* are prepared they will find it easier to come to terms with.)

**4.** The only way to ensure that you achieve your objective is to *make things happen* in such a way that on about 3 June (according to our example – your time scale may of course be different) you will have, not one job offer, but *multiple job offers* (see Chapter 8). To make this happen will require you to maintain a high output of applications which in turn can only be achieved by attacking 100 per cent of your market. The more job leads you can identify the mcre applications you can make which will in turn throw up more interviews. This will also ensure that job offers will occur within the same time frame – which is essential if you are to be in a strong position to negotiate salary and conditions. Negotiate from strength. A job offer in isolation can be a dangerous thing.

---

**The four elements of job searching**

We have, then, identified the four elements which are integral parts of the job-search campaign:

■ **Time**. A finite commodity. Time is money
■ **The market**. The routes through which a job can be found are: speculative, personal contact, agencies and advertised vacancies
■ **The method**. The means by which any one job offer can be generated: application, first interview, second interview
■ **Output**. The determining factor regarding the generation of multiple job offers

---

## The road to success

The aim now is to tie these four elements together in order to devise a meaningful job-search plan. On page 85 we show how such a plan might look in graphic form. Try to look at your campaign as a road made up of building blocks. The road has four lanes, some narrower than others to represent the breakdown of your particular market. The road leads to your final objective – job start.

**Figure 1** represents a 16-week job-search campaign. As yet not all the building blocks are in place. In week one the foundations begin to be laid – all market routes have been 'attacked'. In all, 50 approaches have been made: 25 are what can be described as 'solid applications' ie written approaches direct to employers; the remaining 25 are 'tentative applications' – nine to agencies and 16 via personal contacts.

This initial output has generated ten first interviews which all take place in week four. Because you can't win them all only four second interviews are achieved in week eight. As a result of these second interviews two job offers are achieved in week 12.

**Figure 1** illustrates two important points:

- Imagine what would happen if in week one you attacked only 45 per cent of your market – advertised and agencies ('passive' job-hunting). By week four things look quite rosy – four first interviews. At this stage you might be sorely tempted to cease job-hunting on the basis that at least one of them should result in a job offer. This, as we can see, would be a fundamental error. By week eight there is only one second interview, and by week 12 a *rejection* letter. This is how things could go for anyone adopting an unprofessional job search. Even if that one second interview is successful and results in a job offer by week 12 would it be the *right* job? Would you be in a strong position to negotiate salary? Could you afford the luxury of turning it down? *Time* is fading fast
- The job-search plan as illustrated is *incomplete*. We can see that negative activity has taken place in

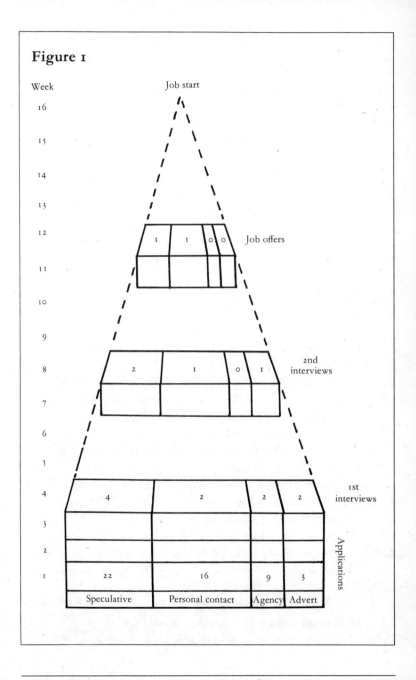

Figure 1

weeks two and three. Should you let this happen the 'knock on' effect will be felt further along the road. No marketing in weeks two and three means no first interviews in weeks five, six and seven, no second interviews in weeks nine, ten and 11, and of course no job offers. The rewards really are commensurate with the effort put in

**Figure 2** shows a more complete job-search plan. The activity generated in week one has been duplicated in week two, even though ten fewer applications have been made – in practice it is quite possible to maintain the level of output if you plan accordingly. Notice that no advertised vacancies have appeared at all in week two – not unusual for the reasons already given. Some of the 11 personal contact approaches may have been 'follow ups' from the original 16 in week one. The 19 further speculative approaches can be generated by extending the geographical boundaries as we shall see later. One week's activity has generated eight first interviews in week five and three second interviews in week nine. The result is one job offer in week 13 – gained from an approach made to an agency.

**Figure 3** shows the overall job-search plan. Thirty-seven applications are made in week three achieving ten first interviews in week six, six second interviews in week ten which result in two job offers in week 14. One of the offers came through an advertised vacancy – which shows that you must not ignore the advertised job market, however narrow that particular part of the road may appear.

To sum up, over an extremely intensive three-week period a total of 127 'applications' were made – by professional job-search standards this is a *modest* total. The complete picture is represented in **Figure 4**.

The road to success has led to multiple job offers within the same time frame (a three-week period). The objective has been achieved. It can *only* be achieved by building the road on a solid

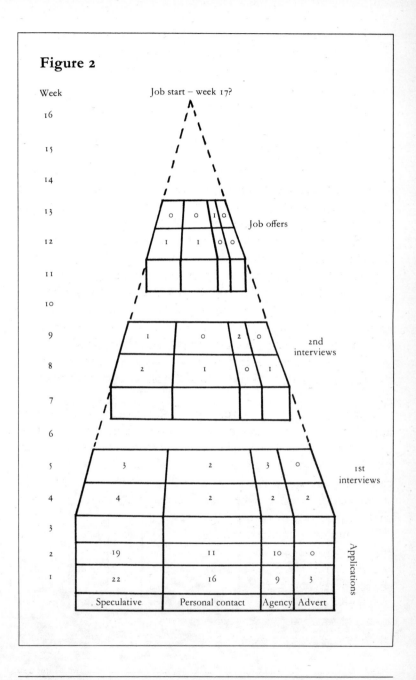

**Figure 2**

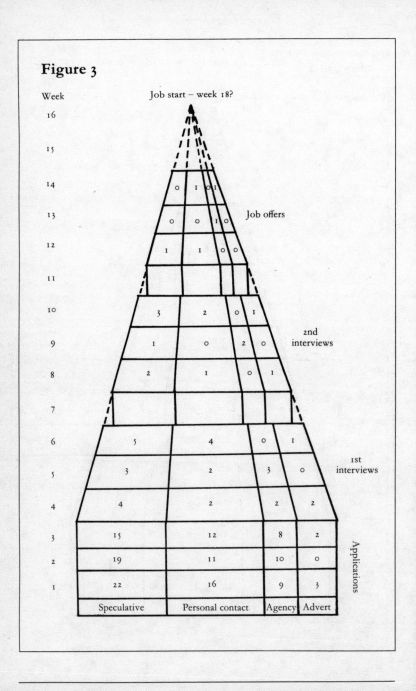

**Figure 3**

Week — Job start – week 18?

| Week | Speculative | Personal contact | Agency | Advert | |
|---|---|---|---|---|---|
| 16 | | | | | |
| 15 | | | | | |
| 14 | o | 1 | o | 1 | |
| 13 | o | o | 1 | o | Job offers |
| 12 | 1 | 1 | o | o | |
| 11 | | | | | |
| 10 | 3 | 2 | o | 1 | |
| 9 | 1 | o | 2 | o | 2nd interviews |
| 8 | 2 | 1 | o | 1 | |
| 7 | | | | | |
| 6 | 5 | 4 | o | 1 | |
| 5 | 3 | 2 | 3 | o | 1st interviews |
| 4 | 4 | 2 | 2 | 2 | |
| 3 | 15 | 12 | 8 | 2 | |
| 2 | 19 | 11 | 10 | o | Applications |
| 1 | 22 | 16 | 9 | 3 | |

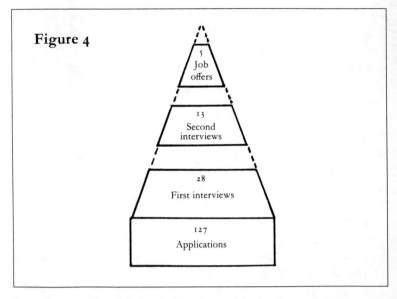

Figure 4

5
Job
offers

13
Second
interviews

28
First interviews

127
Applications

foundation of multiple applications. Notice how, in **Figure 3**, the impression is that in week seven no activity takes place. The reason for this is that in week four attending ten interviews took up much of that week's activity, leaving no time to push out more applications. The 'knock on' effect becomes apparent in week 11 when another fallow period occurs. This is avoidable if you are prepared to work overtime to achieve your objective. Providing you do all the right things you could confidently expect to achieve your objective as a direct result of the intense activity generated in those first three weeks. However, as we shall see, you will have to *manage* and *monitor* the progress of your campaign and if the desired results are not being achieved you must be prepared to continue attacking the market. Notice how in **Figures 2** and **3** each successive week is pushing back the job start date.

## Managing an effective campaign
However good your plan, it will only work if you *manage* it effectively. It is surprising how even professional managers,

who are quite expert at managing projects on behalf of their employer, fail to approach the job search in an equally professional way.

Self-discipline is the key. Job-hunting is a full-time job in itself and has much in common with being self-employed – *you* are the boss and any action has got to be generated from within.

When job-hunting from a position of unemployment we tend to undergo a metamorphosis. The pressure and the stress give rise to all manner of irrational thoughts and woolly ideas which have a negative effect upon campaign management. This is in some part due to fear – fear of the unknown, that road stretching out before us, the 'tyranny of the blank page' upon which we have to write a letter of application. We *need* to apply for jobs but we don't *want* to apply for them. Because of all this we can, if we are not careful, develop some quite noticeable behaviour disorders. Let's take a look now at some of the most typical.

### The victim

Post-Redundancy Stress Disorder (PRSD) is a very real trauma. Low self-esteem, feeling emotionally wounded and not at all keen to start the job search and thus risk further rejection are all symptoms. People in this situation run a high risk of falling prey to the 'vultures' found lurking at the murky end of the job market. If you find yourself in this position, be sure to steer clear of this employment hinterland. Advertisements offering all manner of goodies for only a few hours work a week, commission-only sales jobs and dubious-looking box numbers are strictly out of bounds.

### The perfectionist

The perfectionist takes an almost obsessive interest in the minutae of the job search, typically spending the first week of the campaign gathering together far more resources than necessary. You will certainly need to prepare a work station – a base at home from which to conduct your campaign – but the perfectionist will become attracted, Magpie-like, to all the peripheral nonsense found in the high street stationers, and will frequently return for yet more flexi-curves, stencils and sticky labels. Typically, the perfectionist will spend the next two weeks drafting, re-drafting and producing 15 different versions of the CV. It is certainly not in your interests to despatch sub-standard CVs but the perfectionist will fiddle with it endlessly. This is really an excuse for not having to send any out.

## The tight-wad

The tight-wad is in some respects the opposite of the perfectionist, expecting to conduct an effective campaign on an absolute shoe-string and then express disbelief when not called to an interview. It really is amazing how otherwise professional people will not think twice about spending a great deal of money on social pleasures but become meanness personified when it comes to investing in their own self-marketing. If you consider yourself to be a silk purse, then presenting yourself as if you were a sow's ear will guarantee rejection. In terms of presentation, everything you send out must be *the best example of the work you are capable of producing*. If it is anything less, you will be doing yourself an extreme disservice. Successful job search is not inexpensive, but the tight-wad practices false economy.

## The dust raiser

A veritable cyclone of feverish activity yet producing nothing meaningful. The dust raiser will spend the first two weeks running around from one agency to another and then sit back and produce corporate plans and analyses of past projects while waiting for the phone to ring. Allocate your time to reflect the breakdown of your market as you see it. Spending 95 per cent of your time chasing 20 per cent of your market is not good time-management. The dust raiser is campaign management gone berserk.

### The networker

Networkers have it all in terms of skills, experience, achievements, qualifications and age. They believe, however, that planned job-search is not for them. Networkers are on an altogether higher plane than the rest of us and will spend a month or so travelling into town to have lunch with ex-colleagues. They will express surprise when many of these appointments are cancelled at the last minute. Although they are eminently employable, their complacency will allow their better prepared competitors to pinch the good jobs from under their noses. Few networkers will be reading this book and many will 'retire' early.

### The reactor

The ability to make things happen is not highly developed in the reactor. They tend to 'see what turns up' and successful job-hunters are either 'lucky' or were 'in the right place at the right time'. They forget that both of these things must be preceded by *action*. 'Luck' doesn't just happen. 'Being in the right place at the right time' doesn't just happen. Without action there is nothing, and the more action you can generate the more things are likely to happen. Reactors lose because they snooze.

### The black hole

In their previous life black holes were senior managers who had a secretary or personal assistant to deal with the more mundane aspects of office administration. They have become totally divorced from the need to keep records, details of meetings, or copies of outgoing and incoming correspondence. Black holes are therefore an administrative nightmare. A black hole will be called for an interview three weeks after applying and have no recollection of their original application. It is essential that you keep a running record of applications made, replies received, dates by which follow-ups must be made and appointments kept.

## The researcher

The researcher will soon lose sight of the job-search objective and become irresistably drawn to the mechanics of the job search itself. They will be easily sidetracked by the multitude of resources available to job-seekers at the local library. Certainly cultivate the friendship and expertise of the librarian. They are highly trained and generally relish the opportunity to display *their* skills, but are rarely called upon to do so. The researcher will waste *days* wandering aimlessly around the reference section and gazing in wonder at the microfiche machine.

## The dreamer

It has been calculated that during a 16-week campaign the average job-seeker will consume 640 cups of coffee and 1500 biscuits. The dreamer will exceed this amount by at least 25 per cent. Dreamers feel *guilty* – not only because they have no job but because they are doing nothing about it. Dreamers cannot fall into the 'leafy-lane syndrome' – not for them the honest enjoyment of a round of golf or walking the dog. The dreamer will assume a sedentary position at the work station, polishing the computer and associated peripherals, re-arranging the stationery (for the dreamer is a born-again perfectionist) and staring vacantly at the new fax machine. These bouts of inactivity are interspersed with periods of genuine toil, unfortunately not directed towards the job search. On balance housework is infinitely preferable to writing that application letter. The dreamer will have let standards of dress drop. For both psychological and practical reasons this is bad news. If you dress as if your were going to work you will look professional, perform likewise and maintain self-respect. If you slop around in a pair of jeans and an old jumper, you will look as if you are about to repair the guttering and, even worse, you will probably end up doing so. Dreamers become housebound – rationalizing that they must stay in to take that telephone call should it come. This is nonsense – you are busy and should be out and about. If 'they' want you, they will get you. An employer may be grateful that you were in to take that call, but this will be tinged with a feeling that you have nothing better to do. Dreamers, not unlike dust raisers, always have 'irons in the fire'.

None of the above 'types' are exclusive to each other and you may see yourself in all of them at some time during the job search. The one thing that they all share is a seemingly infinite capacity for self-delusion. The only way to overcome the pitfalls is to establish a weekly timetable geared to achieving the objective. Establishing a *routine* is imperative. If you have been a victim of redundancy, then you have not only lost your job but the routine that went with it – replace this with one of your own. Knowing what you are aiming to achieve on a day-to-day basis gives form and content to the week. Making it up as you go along will make your 'road' a long and winding one.

Set a weekly target of 50 job applications. This may seem a formidable goal to set, but as we rarely achieve *more* than we set out to achieve one thing is for sure, if you set yourself a target of 20 applications a week you won't make 21.

---

### Campaign management checklist

- Do not be side-tracked by 'non jobs', eg sales jobs offering 'commission only'
- Ensure that all your activity is necessary and meaningful
- Do not practice false economy
- Allocate your time to reflect your market breakdown
- Be *pro*active and not *re*active
- Develop an efficient administration system
- Make full use of library resources
- Maintain a high standard of dress
- Establish a weekly timetable
- Set goals

---

## *Monitoring the campaign*

Continuously monitor your performance as you travel along the job-search road. Are you achieving the weekly goal designed to lead you to your objective? Why not? Is your output mediocre? Why? Are you getting many interviews but no job offers? How can this be?

These questions must be answered honestly and objectively. Progress is determined by the successful fusing together of the four job-search elements (plus a fifth which we shall come to in a moment). If you are shaky on any one of these the objective will not be reached. The result must be entirely dependent upon the foundation you have laid in those important first three weeks.

### *Monitoring sequence*

- **Weeks 1 & 2.** Has output been achieved? Have all four market routes been attacked?

- **Week 3.** Output achieved? All market routes attacked? Acknowledgments received of your applications sent during first two weeks? You will by now have received some replies, most of which may be negative. Follow up any which, although negative, were courteous, flattering, or expressed interest in what you are selling – employers' needs can change very quickly. Never allow more than seven working days to elapse without receiving a reply. Chase up potential employers and get them to confirm that they have received your correspondence. This may seem time-consuming and expensive, and you might be tempted not to do it on the basis that 'no news is good news', but in fact 'no news' invariably means 'no action' or 'no receipt'. If they cannot use you then you need to know so that you can get on with more positive things. Failure to follow up means that you will lose control of *time*. Continue this monitoring throughout weeks four, five and six.

- **Week 6.** Output achieved? All market routes attacked? You will by now have attended first interviews. Is the number of interviews a fair reflection of your output? If you have achieved a success rate of less than 15 per cent then questions need to be raised about the fifth element. The fifth element is *quality*. You can achieve output and full market penetration but still get negative results if the quality of your work is poor. Make sure that you are not cutting corners (see Chapter Eight).

■ **Week 7.** By now the building blocks are falling into place and in many respects this is the most intensive time. Not only are you busy attending interviews but you are following all the monitoring procedures outlined previously *and* meeting your output objectives. The pressure and stress will have built up quite considerably. For eight weeks you have been exposed to the tribulations of the job search. You will have come face to face with rejection (in its various guises) on many occasions. In fact, according to our example in *Figure 4* (page 89), rejection has been encountered 114 times by week ten: $(127–28) + (28–13)$. There is no denying that effective job-searching is an emotional roller-coaster. But again, rejection is less traumatic if it coincides with success. 'Linear' job-hunting makes the troughs steeper and deeper.

■ **Weeks 11–14.** The acid test is of course the number of job offers received as a result of second interviews. If you achieve lower than a 40 per cent success rate here then question your interview performance. (We will be seeing In Chapter Nine, however, how rejections after a shortlist interview can be turned into job offers.)

## The Curriculum Vitae

There are widely different views on the nature of the CV. That even 'experts' disagree on how it should be constructed is not surprising since there can be no set format. Why? Because no two 'products' are the same and each CV should be as unique as a fingerprint. For this reason there will be no attempt here to impose a set format and the examples given are no more than that. By completing the Self Analysis Exercise in Chapter Three, you will already have done much of the preparatory work. The self analysis should have given you the answers to the following questions:

1. **What can the product do?** How well do you know what you are selling? Has it been bought before and used effectively by previous customers? Has its full potential been

exploited yet? What qualifications does it have as testimony to its quality? What has it achieved for previous users? This information must now be gathered together as it will form the basis of your 'sales literature' (CV plus accompanying letter).

2. **What *can't* the product do?** Has it remained unused for long periods? Is it a good 'runner' or does it need attention? Has it stayed too long in one place and not really been stretched? You must be aware of your weaknesses so that you can counter any objections at the interview.

You may find it difficult to be objective when constructing your CV – self-portraits are notoriously unreliable. It is even less useful for someone else to do it for you *without having seen you*. The best CVs are produced as the result of a joint effort between yourself and a professional at a face-to-face meeting. This is most likely to achieve the production of a good selling document. CVs by post tend to throw up more of an identikit picture than a representative photograph.

It is unnecessary, and far too time-consuming, to construct a CV for every job applied for. As we have seen, the job search is too intensive for that. Your aim is to prepare a general purpose document that could reasonably be used for all of the positions for which you are likely to apply.

The aim of the CV is to *maximize the number of job interviews achieved*. Once you get an interview the CV has done its job. The initial selection process is not one of selection at all but one of *rejection*, ie buyers will be looking for reasons why they should *not* see certain applicants. Your task is to emphasize why they *must* see you, and to play down any weak points you may have. As the song goes 'Accentuate the positive, eliminate the negative' – this makes the customer more likely to 'latch on to the affirmative'. Logically, if you correctly identify a job that you know you can do and submit your sales literature then subsequent rejection will only happen if something about it has given the prospective employer reason to believe that you will be unsuitable. Although the job search is a 'game' it is not a lottery. There are actions you can take when preparing your CV to minimize the risk of rejection.

# Ten reasons why suitable applicants fail to achieve interviews

## Poor presentation

Like the way you dress for an interview, the way you present yourself on paper reflects the type of person you are. On receipt, your application will receive no more than 60 *seconds* of the prospective employer's time. After 60 seconds a judgment is made – and this judgment will often be made even before a word is read. The logic applied is that if applicants present themselves poorly on paper they are just as likely to present themselves poorly in person and will not be a good advertisement for the employing organization – therefore no interview.

Your CV should be typed, preferably on a word processor, on good quality white A4 paper. A poorly typed CV is little better than a hand-written one. Using a word processor has the additional benefit of allowing for changes in content should they be necessary for a 'one off' application. If possible use a 'daisy wheel' printer rather than a 'dot matrix' one. Until very recently, photocopies, even on good quality paper, were not acceptable. They tended to be immediately identifiable as such and gave the recipient the impression that they were just one of many on your list. Technology has now improved to such an extent that, with a good machine, it is impossible to tell the difference between a photocopy and the original.

There is an argument, not altogether outrageous, which suggests that using paper of a different colour from white will make a CV stand out from those of the competition. Much may depend upon the type of job applied for – seeking a marketing or advertising position, for example, gives a little more licence to innovate. But be careful not to overdo it – a CV on vellum embossed with gold lettering may mark you down as an eccentric or a 'crank'.

A better way of making your CV stand out from the

competition is to despatch it, along with the accompanying letter, in a stiff-backed A4 envelope. It does seem a great pity to construct a well-presented CV only to fold it and shove it into an ordinary envelope. Successful job-searching is often about taking the time, trouble and expense to do things that average job-seekers will put into the 'too difficult' category.

Another way to improve your presentation and make your CV stand out from the competition is to get rid of that ridiculously pretentious term 'Curriculum Vitae'. Average CVs invariably have this emblazoned across the top of the page. You are not selling a Curriculum Vitae, you are selling yourself. It's much better to have your name printed in bold type and centred at the top of the document.

Pay attention to detail. For example, include your post code in your address and give your whole telephone number. Making readers ferret about for your dialling code could be enough to put them off. It should go without saying that attention to detail is particularly important if you are seeking a position that requires that quality (and very few jobs don't) – the reader is bound to look for evidence of it in your application.

Above all, make sure your CV is *clear*. Avoid going overboard on underlining and superfluous use of headings such as 'name', 'address', 'marital status', 'nationality', 'telephone number' – your telephone number is unlikely to be mistaken for your credit card number. Apart from anything else, space is at a premium because you will be aiming to get your CV on a *maximum of two sides of A4 paper* – don't squander it.

Should you send a photograph with your CV? Never! A well-presented CV can be effectively destroyed by an average-looking photograph – and most photographs are just that.

Finally, there must of course be no errors of spelling or typing. If you have typed it yourself then get someone to check it for you – if you have made a mistake you may be the last person to spot it.

## Too old

There is little doubt that age can be an obstacle to getting the right job. Nothing is more frustrating than knowing you have what it takes to contribute yet being denied the opportunity because the calendar, to some, implies otherwise. At the application stage there are certain actions you can take to limit the damage. It is really a question of saying 'Yes, age may be against me but what am I going to do about it?'

Firstly, it might be useful to question your own prejudices relating to age – one can be both a victim of ageism and an unknowing supporter of it. After all, the enemy is not so much age but *attitudes* towards it. Applicants' negative attitudes about there own age are frequently detectable in their written applications. Typically, an application letter will read: 'Although I am over the age limit for this position . . .'. Such a statement can clearly indicate to the reader that the writer sees age as a problem – in which case it will be.

CVs tend to give undue emphasis to age, marital status, number of children (and ages of same) – all of which, for most jobs, should have no bearing whatsoever on suitability. Because such details are highlighted at the beginning of the document, the reader is almost forced to give them undue attention and is *influenced* before having had an opportunity to read the more pertinent information.

For this reason, you should put *all* personal details other than name, address and telephone number at the end of your CV – unless placing them first will, for some obscure reason, increase your chances of getting that interview. Always give your date of birth rather than stating your actual age. If age is important to employers let them work it out for themselves.

There are more subtle ways in which age can work against you. For example, if you make a statement on your CV to the effect that you have '30 years experience of production engineering' you are, quite understandably, trying to highlight your experience, but to the reader you are also highlighting the fact that you are probably over 50 years of age. In any case, trying to sell experience in terms of time can be a big mistake: it doesn't tell the reader *how good* you are at the job, only how long you have been in it. You can also be a victim of your own pride. You may be very proud of the fact that you have 'spent a lifetime' in the shipping industry but a statement to that effect will give the reader the impression that you have already made your funeral arrangements.

Age itself isn't a problem. The problem arises from *prejudices* and *perceptions* about age. There are people who tend to view anyone over a certain age as being in their *declining* years, as being worn out with nothing to give and no enthusiasm for anything. This is clearly ludicrous, particularly as many 20-year-olds could fit that description. Your task is to avoid *reinforcing* the existing prejudices, by refusing to conform to the stereotype. What you are is reflected by how you look, how you behave and what you say – if it looks like a duck, walks like a duck and makes a noise like a duck – it's a duck.

## Salary

The whole area of salary is fraught with problems and pitfalls for the unwary. In the private sector *always assume that salaries are negotiable*. A salary is either negotiable or it is not and the only way to find out is to start negotiating – but not yet. 'Don't cross your bridges until you come to them' could well be the battle cry for all job-seekers. Putting your salary on your CV has the following risks:

■ Employers will see that your present/most recent salary is more than they are willing to pay. Although you *might* be willing to drop your salary, you may not get an interview to discuss the point. Employers are, not unnaturally, often reluctant to take people on at a lower salary than they were earning before. They might feel that you are using them as a 'stop-gap' and will soon become disenchanted with the job, or may feel that they would be wasting your time by offering you an interview

■ Employers will see that your present/most recent salary is a good deal less than they are willing to pay. In this case you may get through to an interview but have seriously weakened your bargaining position – if the salary is negotiable they will use your present salary as their starting point. Alternatively, they may not offer you an interview because they think you are too 'lightweight' for the job

■ You could be giving very misleading information. Your present salary is not in itself an accurate reflection of *what the job is worth to you*. You may have perks such as a company car, mortgage subsidy, free/subsidized lunches, medical insurance, non-contributory pension etc – all of which go to make up your Total Remuneration Package (TRP). Your present *salary* may be higher than the employer can go, but their TRP may be greater than your present one. Alternatively, your present salary may be a good deal lower than the one they might be offering but your TRP may be greater, particularly if there are no 'add ons' to their salary. When advertising, employers have an irritating habit of not declaring *their* TRP (often for understandable reasons) but asking you to declare *yours*. The financial arrangement you have negotiated with your present employer is a personal matter between you and them – strictly speaking it is no one else's business. If you feel that you really *must* declare your salary then do so on the accompanying letter – it has no place on your CV

## Failure

Given that employers employ people to get results it naturally follows that CV evidence indicating *failure* to get results will seriously work against you. Nearly everyone who has had the courage to attempt something can remember at least one occasion when it hasn't worked, so failure is not something to get obsessed about. It is really a question of balance and degree. Failing an examination, for example, is not the end of the world. Indeed, if you tried again, and passed, you may get a great deal of mileage out of it – it shows that you are determined and not put off by set-backs. But the CV is the wrong place to get such points across – the interview is the place to do that. Remember a failed objective is no more than that. What is interesting is how the reader of your CV can quite easily get an impression that you are a failure by reading what are, to you, innocent statements. Let us look at a few:

■ **'Marital Status: Divorced'.** It is surprising how often people put this on their CV, and of course compound the error by giving it pride of place at the top! Whichever way you look at it divorce is a statement of failure which can instantly give you the mark of Cain. If you are still married then say so. If you are divorced then you are single; if you are separated you are married.

■ **Job titles.** Misleading job titles can also be harmful and may indicate failure even if you were a resounding success. Consider the following 'career pattern':

Present job      'Marketing Manager'
Previous job    'Senior Marketing Manager'
Previous job    'Marketing Manager'

Now there can be a number of perfectly good reasons why you moved from 'Senior Marketing Manager' *back*(?) to 'Marketing Manager'. Trying to give a lengthy explanation on a CV (or accompanying letter) will probably do you more harm than good, but if you leave it as it is who could blame the reader for thinking 'He/she was promoted but obviously couldn't take the pace'? A job title in one company can mean something quite different in another, so have no hesitation in *changing* past job titles if you feel they might give your potential employer a totally misleading impression of you, what you did, or the circumstances surrounding your job changes. If necessary, you can explain at the interview – if you adhere blindly to previous job titles you may not be at interviews to discuss them.

Stating that you have a 'clean driving licence' could indicate to some that at one stage it was *not* clean. 'Full driving licence' is the appropriate term, but then only necessary if it is a requirement of the job.

■ **Unfinished business**. Think carefully before indicating that you have started something but not finished it: no one likes a 'quitter'. At the interview (should you be successful) little respect will be given to the fact that you had the initiative, enthusiasm and self-motivation to study part-time for a professional qualification. What *will* be questioned is the fact that you failed to complete it. As far as the CV is concerned it is worse to have started something and given up than not to have started at all.

## Prejudice

Whether we care to admit it or not we all have prejudices. We make judgments on people based upon their age, sex, appearance etc. Prejudice comes into play most strongly at the interview, but there is a particular part of the CV which can have a much stronger influence on employers than some applicants think. This is the section you might call 'hobbies' or (preferably) 'interests'.

It is up to you to decide upon the importance of such a section, but if you decide to include it take care. Many 'recruiters' are interested in your activities outside the working arena because it gives them a clearer idea of the 'whole person'. Unfortunately it can also provide the fuel to fire their prejudices. I have heard more than one employer remark that he would not choose to interview anyone who put 'golf' or 'sailing' on their CV. The rationale for this seems to be that they are both time-consuming interests and as such are incompatible with the full-time commitment expected from employees.

Some prejudices arise from experience and if an employer has had a bad experience with past employees disappearing early to get to the coast then this would, not unnaturally, colour their feelings on this point. This issue is complicated by the fact that in some organizations the ability to play golf or sail is virtually a pre-requisite to working for them. You might take the view that if they feel *that* strongly about it (either way) you don't want to work for them anyway. An admirable sentiment – except that such prejudice is not usually a reflection of company policy, simply that of one individual whose job it is to weed out CVs.

A list of someone's interests can also be extremely boring. Many applicants put down an interest not because it is one but because they can't think of anything else to put. This is clearly ludicrous – any good interviewer would probe this at the interview and discover it to be a facade. Countless job applicants have lost their credibility at an interview through their inability to support their CV 'interests'. 'Reading' is a typical example. If you put down 'reading' then be prepared for the question 'Who is your favourite author?' or 'What are you reading at the moment?'. If this part of your CV comes across as 'hype' the recipient may well deduce that the rest of it is too.

The overall effect of your *combination* of interests can also influence the reader (for better or worse). Consider the following combinations:

'Reading. Philately. Listening to music.'

Nothing is necessarily wrong with any of these, but should the employer be seeking someone who is a good team player then such a combination of interests might indicate otherwise. They are all *solitary* pursuits – is the applicant a loner? In addition, they could be described as somewhat *passive*, which, if a certain degree of 'dynamism' is called for, might not help the applicant.

'Hockey. Swimming. Athletics.'

Again, there is nothing particularly wrong with any one of these. This person is probably a good team player and must be fit but the lack of cultural pursuits might mark them down as a philistine, the importance of which would depend upon the prejudices of the prospective employer and the type of position applied for.

'Reading. DIY. Listening to music.'

If there were a Richter Scale for measuring pure unadulterated *tedium* this combination would register ten.

'Rock climbing. Hang Gliding. Free-fall parachuting.'

Should this person achieve an interview one of the first questions will be 'Have you had many days off through sickness?' Remember that the customer is considering investing *money* in you and no one likes to see their investment (literally) plummet. If the character needed to indulge in such pastimes is relevant to the job then certainly include it. If, however, you are seeking something less arduous then keep such pursuits to yourself, or at least until the interview.

As with any other part of the CV, the emphasis must be on *success*, *achievement*, *skills*, *transferable skills* or anything *relevant* which demonstrates your *uniqueness*. Consider this combination:

'School Governor. Social Club Treasurer. Successfully established Sunday league soccer team.'

This gives a revealing picture of the 'whole person' and *implies* the existence of a range of useful qualities, such as being community-minded, a good 'mixer', a 'self-starter', a good leader and team player, an achiever and a proactive rather than reactive or passive person. Even if the reader does not form such a conclusion (perhaps through lack of perception or time) these are all skills and qualities that can be sold at the interview. They also provide *evidence* either to *support* other skills and experiences on the CV or *compensate* for the lack of them.

The basic question to ask yourself is: 'Are my activities sufficiently interesting to increase my chances of achieving an interview, or could they actually *prevent* me from doing so?' If they are unlikely to do a good selling job for you, leave them out.

## Too good for the job

Being *perceived* by employers as being too 'heavyweight' for the job is often more frustrating than not being good enough. If you are judged not to be experienced/qualified enough you will normally receive a rejection letter saying so, but you will rarely get an explanation if you are *too* good. Without such feedback, therefore, you will have to do the detective work yourself. If they have declined to offer you an interview and you feel that 'being too good' is the reason then ask yourself two questions:

1. 'Are they right, *am* I too good for the job?'
2. 'Are they wrong but am I over-selling?'

If the answer to the first question is 'yes' then the employer has probably done you a favour. You are clearly lowering your sights and in danger of taking the wrong job. You may have sound reasons for wanting to move down a few gears, but it can be quite difficult to convince employers that you really would be content to shed status and responsibility. Firstly, they may feel that after a few months you would become restless and start seeking better jobs elsewhere. Secondly, they may feel that your continued presence may become uncomfortable, or even threatening – doctors don't like their nurses to be *too* intelligent.

If you are certain that you are *not* too 'heavyweight' for the job and that you *are* aiming at the right market, then look again at your CV. Over-selling is just as dangerous as under-selling, but more difficult to identify. Obvious points to look out for are salary (see page 101) and job titles (page 103). Be prepared to alter job titles in a 'downwards' as well as an 'upwards' direction if you believe they might be misleading. Over the past ten years certain titles have become notoriously abused and devalued, eg 'consultant', 'executive', 'director'. Your present job title may be 'Operations Director' but is it really very different from 'Operations Manager'? Increasingly, employers are giving their employees fancy job titles to make them feel good, but which in essence are no more than euphemisms, so be careful not to over-value your position.

Although you must stress good selling points, be careful not to overdo it or you could easily come across as being boastful and conceited: the dividing line between confidence and 'cockiness' is a very thin one. Employers may interpret the words and phrases you use in an entirely unexpected way. 'Troubleshooter', for instance, is creeping into CVs rather a lot these days, but for some it is too close to 'trouble*maker*' for comfort.

Having 'too many' qualifications can be just as much of a problem as having too few. This is a sound justification for putting your qualifications at the end of the CV rather than the beginning, unless you are seeking a position in academia. Should you be the proud possessor of a PhD, for some jobs you may need to play this down rather than sell it strongly. Placing the title 'Dr' next to your name at the top could put some people off. This also applies to officers in the services seeking civilian employment. 'Major John Brown' may sound less than endearing to some civilian employers.

Applicants seeking scientific/technical/academic positions are particularly prone to being perceived as 'too heavyweight' by employers. This perception is often unwittingly encouraged by such applicants through their insistence upon detailing every item of equipment ever used by them and every published paper. These are of course important details – so important in some cases that the offer of an interview may hinge on their inclusion – but keep such information *separate*. Do not allow it to invade the CV itself.

Training courses can also hinder rather than help an application. It is not unusual for applicants to include on their CV a list of training courses they have attended when working for previous employers. This in itself is not necessarily a hazard since many courses are very useful and extremely expensive. Potential employers may then be very relieved to escape the expense of sending an employee on a particular course. But it can be double-edged: the list of courses attended by some applicants is so extensive that the employer cannot but wonder how little time the applicant actually spent at work. 'Professional course attenders' are a well-recognized breed of job applicant. If you are tempted to include such information then question the importance/relevance of each course and be selective.

## Lack of experience

Indicating that you do not have the necessary experience for the job is frequently no more than the result of selling the wrong things on the CV. The reader is, more precisely, looking for *relevant* experience, ie particular aspects of your past/present experience which are likely to be useful in *fulfilling their needs*. CVs have an alarming tendency to confuse the reader by drawing attention to *irrelevancies*. These irrelevancies act as a smoke-screen which, particularly in long-winded CVs, hides the fact that you do indeed have relevant experience.

For example, many applicants unwittingly make the mistake of selling *their previous employers* rather than themselves. Much valuable space is devoted to giving a blow-by-blow account of a previous employer's strategy, restructuring/ reorganizing, acquisitions and policy, all of which might be interesting should the reader have both the time and inclination to read it, but bears no direct relevance at all to the applicant's suitability for the job. In addition, inadvertently divulging privileged information about previous employers is unlikely to endear you to others – they may offer you an interview to find out even more about their competitors but you will pay the price for your indiscretion.

Irrelevancies can also creep in if you are moving from one 'industry' to another quite different one. If, for example, your most recent experience has entailed managing the distribution of 'white goods' (freezers, washing machines etc) and you are just as likely to be applying for jobs specializing in 'brown goods' (televisions, videos etc), then peppering your CV with references to specific items of kitchen furniture is unlikely to enhance your case. That you have experience in managing the distribution of one type of goods is not *immediately* and *directly* relevant to *where you want to be* ie managing the distribution of another type. The relevant and common factor is that they are both 'electrical consumer products' – it is this that should appear on the CV and not references to the products themselves.

Steer away from any references which may encourage the reader to say 'We are not in that line of business, therefore this is all irrelevant experience'. Getting the fact across that you have relevant experience requires you to be *clear* and *concise*. Refuse to hide behind 'woolly' words and phrases which continually seem to crop up on CVs but which mean very little to the reader – words like 'Wide', 'Broad', 'Involved', 'Dealing with . . .'. How wide? How broad? How were you involved? How did you 'deal with' customer problems? Did you *resolve* them? What skills did you use in resolving them? It is here that we begin to see the importance of the Skills Analysis Exercise in Part 1.

If the right job is one which allows you to broaden your career then by definition it must give you something *new*. This means that it must allow you to undertake *new* responsibilities which give you *new* experiences which in turn allow you to develop *new* skills and the opportunity to *achieve* new things. It naturally follows that you will be seeking a job for which you do not possess all of the required experience (although, as we have said, you may already possess the *skill* to do it). Looking at it another way, if you are applying for a position for which you have all of the required experience, then you are probably in danger of going for the *wrong* job (not *again*!). For this reason, you should not be unduly concerned by the experience you *lack* as long as you can sell the experience that you *have*.

Highlighting irrelevancies on the CV will also happen if you give too much importance to your earliest jobs. Employers are only likely to be interested in what you have been doing during the past few years: the further back you go the less relevant your experience will be. For early jobs it is only necessary to give the name of your employer and a job title. Because your most recent work is likely to be the most relevant you must give it priority. This means that (unless you have a valid reason for doing otherwise) your career progression must be outlined in reverse chronological order, ie your most recent job first and working backwards through to your earliest job. Making the reader wade through 20 years of irrelevancies can seriously diminish the appetite for reading any further. It may well be that your relevant experience is dispersed throughout your career but punctuated by periods of irrelevant experience (in fact, that statement would neatly sum up the careers of many of us). If so, the *functional* style of CV (see page 123) would probably be most appropriate for you – the great bonus of using this style is that experience is taken out of its historical context.

There is little doubt, then, that lack of relevant experience can impair your chances of getting an interview, and often quite rightly so – either you have enough of the right experience or you don't. But applicants will often fail at this hurdle, not because they do not have the requisite amount of relevant experience but through their failure to sell it in the right way. Who can blame a busy employer for failing to reach the right conclusion in 60 seconds?

## Job-hopper

Although you may have changed employers quite regularly the 'job-hopping' criticism should only be levelled at you if it is clear that there is no logical pattern to your moves. In these circumstances employers may conclude that you are shiftless, indecisive, lacking in direction and a square peg who always seems to squeeze into a round hole. Such criticism can of course be very unfair. Fate does sometimes deal a poor hand and such things as changing family circumstances can override and damage career objectives. Most sensible employers would not be unduly worried about one period of employment outside your chosen career path. Job-hopping is about consistent career abuse, ie when consecutive job changes bear no identifiable relation to each other.

If you *are* a job-hopper the good news is that it isn't a terminal disease. You simply haven't found the right vehicle through which your latent abilities and potential can be tapped. But from a practical point of view there is little you can do to offset this on the CV – in one way or another you must tell employers where you have worked, what you did and when. The more job changes you have had (whether logical or otherwise) the more 'messy' your CV is likely to look. This can be offset by using the functional CV and giving less priority to dates of employment.

Traditionally, CVs have tended to place undue emphasis on this by having dates of employment down the left hand side of the page. Because we read from left to right it is the dates we see first. This can lead to instant confusion and detract from the more pertinent information. Put the dates on the *right* of the page – after all, *what* you have done is more important than *when* you did it.

Your desire not to be seen as a job-hopper may tempt you to state your 'reasons for leaving' previous jobs, but why you left one employer and joined another is a bridge to be crossed at the interview – it is easier to explain your motives at a face-to-face meeting.

Generally, be very cautious about including your 'objective' or 'position sought' on your CV. Although there is nothing essentially wrong in doing this for 'one-off' CVs aimed at a particular job, for a general purpose CV it is infuriating to see that your 'objective' does not quite fit the bill on every occasion during an intensive job search. If you do have an objective which fits the bill every time then it is probably so vague as to be useless. However, because job-hopping is a sign that one has perhaps in the past had no clear objective, it can be a good idea to compensate for this by stating clearly and confidently what your objective is *now*.

## Too young

Being considered 'too young' for a job is just as much of an anachronism as being considered too old. It is meaningless in the context of employment – either a person is *competent* enough to do the job or they are not. Lack of skill or ability can render both 'young' and 'old' applicants incompetent but age itself cannot.

Some jobs do require a level of maturity not often found in someone below a certain age. A problem arises because some people (and not necessarily the employing organization), through their own prejudices and preconceptions, believe that maturity/ability can *never* be found in someone below a certain age. During an interview a 'young' applicant can challenge those prejudices and change those perceptions – unfortunately, the interview may not be forthcoming *because* of the very existence of that prejudice. Personal insecurity makes some individuals within organizations see 'youth' as a potential threat to their position.

Once you are inside an organization and seeking promotion it is easier to change the perceptions of others – getting results is one of the strongest arguments against entrenched attitudes. If you *do* lack the maturity/ability/skill required by the employer, this will inevitably show up in your application. If you *don't* lack these qualities then you should be able to produce a quality CV to suggest as much. This is done not by referring in any way to your age (that would be just highlighting a 'weakness') but by displaying *belief* and a confident self-image. As with the 'too old' objection, it is a matter of refusing to conform to the stereotype. Ensure that your CV is a strong selling document and in no way servile or lacking in conviction.

## The 'Empty Taxi' syndrome

'An empty taxi pulled up and the applicant got out.' Perhaps the most common reason for rejection is the 'empty taxi' CV. This is a CV which conveys nothing to the reader – at least nothing which will encourage them to recommend an interview. A good CV should convey the message 'Look at me, I am worth seeing'. The 'empty taxi' conveys a quite different message – 'I'm only applying on the off-chance that you might see me, then I will *really* be able to tell you how bad I am'.

The 'empty taxi' applicant lacks assurance, has no idea what is being sold (or indeed that anything has to be sold) and fails to reassure the reader. We have already seen the need for self analysis, the exploration of 'self' which helps to identify who you are and your needs in terms of a job. Once this is achieved the emphasis during the job search must shift towards showing a greater understanding and awareness of *the needs of the employer*. For many applicants such a shift fails to take place; the job search remains self-centred. This is reflected by CVs which simply list a sequence of employers, job titles and responsibilities – with no indication at all of skills, achievements or personal qualities. In addition, accompanying letters contain the 'I want' and 'I am now looking for' phrases which are anathema to anyone involved in recruitment.

A good employer will of course be interested in your needs in terms of career objectives and salary. But these matters will only be addressed once clear signals have been received from you that you have something to *offer*. 'Empty taxis' fail to convey these signals.

To understand the importance of this is to realize the one fundamental need possessed by *all* recruiters ie *the need to keep their job*. Those charged with the onerous responsibility of selecting the right person are required to tread a thin and precarious line. Not all are trained in those techniques designed to increase the probability of selecting round pegs for round holes. Getting it right is their primary objective, largely because the cost of getting it wrong is loss of credibility with peers and senior staff and, should it happen too often, loss of a job. This applies just as much to agencies. They are paid by employers to select and recommend suitable applicants; they need to get it right because they want employers to continue providing them with business – protecting their client base is the number one priority.

The customer, whether employer or agency, therefore needs *reassurance* from you, *in writing*, that you have what it takes to fulfil their needs. Early on in the rejection process, the customer (who may at this stage be represented by someone quite junior in the organization) will cast aside all CVs which fail the reassurance test. It is at this stage that all the 'empty taxis' are sidelined.

It is not good enough to present them with a ten-page chronology of your life and a 'pleasant' accompanying letter – this is giving them far too much work to do. The reader needs hard facts to present to senior managers. They must be able to say 'I think we should see this person *because* . . .'.

So there are the ten most common reasons why even suitable applicants fail to achieve the first step along the road to success. You will now need to construct a CV which avoids *all* of these faults.

Firstly, let us look at the layout of the CV. A more than acceptable layout would comprise the ten elements which are shown in **Figure 5**.

### The ten elements of your CV – action checklist

**1. Name.**

- Print your name in *bold type* at centre top of CV
- No need to use your full or legal names. Use the name you wish to be addressed by at the interview

**2. Address.**

- Top left of CV or directly beneath your name at centre
- Pay attention to detail – include your post-code

**Figure 5**

1. NAME

2. ADDRESS                    3. TELEPHONE

4. PROFILE

5. KEY SKILLS/ACHIEVEMENTS/EXPERIENCES

6. CAREER                    7. DATES

8. EDUCATION

9. PERSONAL

10. INTERESTS

## 3. Telephone number.
- Top right of CV
- Give the full dialling code
- Give your work and home numbers if you can

## 4. Profile.
- Make it brief – no more than three sentences
- Describe yourself as *you* wish – don't stick to previous job titles if they mislead
- Does it give the reader an indication of where you want to be in terms of a job? (This does not mean that you have to state an overall objective)

## 5. Key skills/achievements/experiences.
- Return to the Self Analysis Exercise (pages 28–48). Which skills came out on top in the matrix? These are what you are likely to be selling
- Give no more than six key skills etc
- Use the right 'action words' to describe them
- Do not include dates
- Remember the importance of *transferable skills*

## 6. Career.
- Start with your present/most recent job and work backwards
- Use 'telex' style sentences – cut the waffle. Avoid using the 'first person singular'. Space is at a premium and a continuous narrative style is uneconomical; you also run the risk of boring the reader to tears. Omitting all the 'I' references improves clarity and power. After all, the reader knows that the CV is about *you* so there's no need to keep saying so
- Quantify your *responsibilities* eg number, volume, value, area, distance etc. Quantify your *achievements*: if you increased sales say by how much; if you re-organized a department so that it needed fewer people then give a percentage. This precise information provides the *evidence* they need to assess your capabilities
- Avoid using 'jargon' or 'buzz words' which may have been used in your present/last company. Many working environments breed a sub-culture where language nuances play a great part. There is a danger that these will creep into

your CV and although it makes sense to you what will an
outsider make of it?
- Keep it brief. You are fishing for an interview and this is
  your bait – don't overload the hook. A long CV will be
  given short shrift
- Give less space to irrelevant early jobs
- Always write in the present tense, even when describing
  past jobs. Using the 'ing' as opposed to the 'ed' can give
  past experiences more immediacy

## 7. Dates.
- Put all dates on the right. Placing them on the left gives
  them an emphasis they do not deserve
- Forget 'months' – they are irrelevant and untidy on the page
- Do not leave years unaccounted for

## 8. Education.
- Omit examination failures and mediocre grades
- Give priority to most relevant qualifications eg if you have a
  degree there is no need to spell out each 'O' level or GCSE
  qualification
- Be selective when mentioning training courses attended

## 9. Personal.
- Marital status: 'married' or 'single' – not 'divorced' or
  'separated'
- Put 'date of birth' not 'age'

## 10. Interests.
- Only include interests which are different, intriguing, or
  which indicate transferable skills
- Assess the overall impact of your interests

## *Case study 1 – Pauline Dixon*

Page 119 shows an example of a one-page CV which
incorporates all ten elements. Is there enough information here
for the reader to make a judgment regarding her suitability for
interview? The answer is 'probably not'. This is quite
deliberate. It is essential to understand that the CV *rarely travels*

# PAULINE DIXON

6 Worcester Drive, Budely, Yorkshire. YK7 5HF.          0853 68495

MARKETING/PR EXECUTIVE with comprehensive retail/wholesale experience in the UK, Europe and USA.

Key skills include:

* Managing profitable operation of multi-product retail outlets.
* Promoting exclusive range of products worldwide.
* Liaising with foreign suppliers, government agencies and local authorities.
* Recruiting and training of staff.

## CAREER

Imperial Porcelain Company, York.                    1980–91
*Company Trading Manager*

– Product promotion at 3 sites. Development of each as tourist attractions.
– Profitable operation of 6 site shops.
– Achieving sales targets and controlling operating costs.
– Establishing high street retail outlets.
– Advertising budget of £200k. Turnover £4m. Staff of 85.

Navy, Army & Air Force Institutes.                   1970–80
*District Manager*

– Managing 20 outlets in UK and Germany covering retail, wholesale, licensed and catering trades.
– Forecasting sales.
– Providing entertainment activity in clubs.
– Liaising with Services, PSA and suppliers.
– Turnover £3.5m. Staff of 120.

Macey's Department Store, New York.                  1965–70
*PA to Vice-President Sales*

## EDUCATION

Budely Girls' Grammar School. 3 'A' levels, 1 'S' level.
Pitmans Central College, London. Higher Secretarial Diploma.
Studying for Open University Degree.

## PERSONAL

Date of Birth 12.8.44      Single.

## INTERESTS
Obtained Private Pilot's Licence in 1981. Theatre, Music, Tennis.

*alone*. More often than not it will be accompanied by a letter, the importance of which is totally disregarded by most job-seekers in the mistaken belief that the CV should do all the work. The CV on its own is unlikely to yield an interview. It is the combination of CV and accompanying letter which does this. The CV represents 50 per cent of your sales literature. The accompanying letter *complements* the CV and represents the other 50 per cent. The letter will be different for every application and the CV will be the same. This allows you to have a brief, general purpose CV. Anything in your past which may be particularly relevant to a specific job, and which does not stand out (or even appear) on the CV, can be emphasized in the letter. This is why it is, or should be, misleading when we look at a CV in isolation – we are only seeing half of the picture.

The 'profile' of this CV is a good one. Pauline has declined to call herself a 'Company Trading Manager' – her most recent job title. She is prepared to describe herself in her own way and does not allow previous employers to put her 'in a box'. Of course, if she were not prepared to travel outside the UK there would be little point in stressing her international experience so strongly. The word 'profitable' is used in the 'key skills' – an eye-catching word for any employer in the private sector.

According to the CV Pauline is unemployed (1980–91). If you are still in work don't give the impression that you might not be – '1980-Present' would, in such a case, be the correct way to put it. There is no 'waffle' in the CV. This is avoided by using the 'telex' style and omitting the 'I' reference – this makes the reader's job so much easier.

There is plenty of evidence to suggest that Pauline is single-minded, self-motivated, pro-active and confident – international experience at an early age, actually *doing something* to improve her educational qualifications and a private pilot's licence. All in all there are few reasons to reject this application and plenty of reasons to see her in order to *find out more*.

## Case study 2 – Bill Johnstone

A good CV but one which could have been improved with a little more thought. Much will of course depend upon the type of job Bill is seeking. He may feel that his age limits his options, and this might be the reason he has chosen not to include a profile. He does have nearly 20 years experience in security and safety and he does sell this in a prominent position in the CV. We must assume then that this is the area in which he will be concentrating his search. This being the case, a profile stating that he is a 'Fully experienced Security/Safety specialist with management and supervisory skills' would have told the reader more directly where he was coming from *and* given a stronger indication of where he wanted to be. It would have given the CV more *conviction* and at the same time played down the fact that he is currently a Chief Security Manager (thus avoiding the 'too good for the job' objection).

Bill could have made room for the profile by eliminating the descriptions of his duties as a 'Caulker Burner' and 'Demolition Supervisor'. The job titles would have sufficed since the safety implications of these jobs would have been self-evident. He is very unlikely to move back into the demolition business so there is no point in making a meal of it.

He uses the right 'action words' but (like so many others) slips back into the past tense (from 'Supervis*ing*' and 'Organiz*ing*' to 'Maintain*ed*' and 'Investigat*ed*').

'Carried out random/regular personal and vehicle searches' is left as a vague statement. What does this mean? How accurate a description is it of what Bill actually did? As the Chief Security Manager one would have expected Bill's six security officers to have *carried out* the searches.

If you select the wrong word then the reader will *read* the wrong word. This in turn will leave them with an inaccurate description of *what you did*.

# BILL JOHNSTONE

62 Methuen Road
Horndean
Worcester
WC4 6FS
Worcester (0833) 6532

## CAREER

BLACKWOOD ELECTRONICS Ltd – Worcester     1974–
Present

*Chief Security Manager* responsible for total security of 9 acre high
risk warehouse and distribution site employing 275 personnel with
stock valued at up to £70 million.
- Supervising 6 security officers and organising shift rotas to provide
  24 hour security cover.
- Organising site fire drills. Liaising with Chief Fire Officer and
  carrying out joint site inspections. Maintaining fire equipment.
- Maintained First Aid and Ambulance facilities. Investigated all
  accidents and identified safety hazards.
- Carried out random/regular personal and vehicle searches.
- Investigated incidents liaising with police and management.

HOMELEIGH GROUP Ltd – Hereford     1971–74

*Security and First Aid Officer* supervising 3 security and 2 ambulance
room staff.
- Working on a three shift system.
- Looking after on-site car parking.

WATSON & HUGHES LTD – Liverpool     1964–71

*Demolition Supervisor*
- Demolition of factories (mainly steel).
- Training 9 men in safety and hazard identification.
- Looking after burning equipment and oxy-acetaline.

TFF HOLDINGS Ltd – Liverpool     1954–64

*Caulker Burner*
- Operating electronic burning machines.

NATIONAL SERVICE – Paratrooper and Medic     1951–54

SEWARD CONSTRUCTION Ltd – Glasgow     1946–51

*Shipyard Worker*

## PERSONAL

Date of Birth: 4.8.30     Single     Full driving licence

## Case study 3 – Martin Hodge

This is an example of a 'functional CV'. This style is particularly suitable for anyone whose career or 'experiences' can be neatly described under two or more functional headings. The problem with the chronological format is that you can sometimes be constrained by dates. This makes it difficult to sell something highly relevant but which may have taken place some years previously. The great benefit of the functional style is that skills, experiences and achievements are taken out of their historical context – there is no obvious link between these things and the employer. The 'employment history' is there for information but kept separate. This style is also useful because, with the aid of a word processor, the emphasis of different functions can be changed to suit the occasion, eg in this example 'Marketing' could be relegated to second place below 'Management' if the job for which he is applying has a strong management bias.

Notice how the oblique (/) is used. As long as you don't overdo it this is a useful way of avoiding the repetitious 'and'. Similarly, the ampersand is useful.

The use of *intrigue* is also an effective tool. In fact, a good CV should always be intriguing – the reader should be intrigued enough to want to see you to find out more. This is achieved by alluding to things but declining to expand upon them. Martin's CV achieves this on a number of occasions: 'Editing prestigious business magazine.' Which one? 'Marketing of a unique building/engineering product.' What was it? What made it unique? 'Promoting the sale of recovered valuable materials.' Recovered from where? What materials? How valuable? 'To high net worth international clients.' How rich? Who? A good CV should be *provocative*.

# MARTIN HODGE

27 Court Road
Whitchurch
Manchester
MC9 4EL                                             038 8546

A MARKETING SPECIALIST with a flair for diplomacy and
communicating/negotiating on a world-wide basis at all levels.

## KEY SKILLS/ACHIEVEMENTS

* English/French/Portuguese: Trilingual; Italian:Spoken.
* Initiating new business/development ideas and seeing them through
  to successful completion.
* Creating new departments and highly professional teams to meet
  new business challenges.
* Efficient management of all marketing functions and liaison with
  other key managers, both internally and externally.

## EXPERIENCE

*Marketing:*     Creating, launching and overall marketing of a new
                 international business centre. Planning,
                 implementing and controlling marketing
                 communications strategies for EEC countries.
                 Generating new product ideas. Researching of UK
                 and international markets. Briefing advertising
                 agencies and monitoring effectiveness of
                 campaigns. Devising promotional literature
                 (corporate brochures/direct mail shots). Editing of
                 prestigious business magazine. Marketing of a
                 unique building/engineering product to
                 international construction companies. Promoting
                 the sale of recovered valuable materials to high net
                 worth international clients.

*Management:*    Managing the retail, office, sales and technical
                 facilities for the French branch of a multi-national
                 American security organisation. Co-ordinating/
                 organising the workloads of teams of line managers
                 and reporting directly to the CEO. Budget
                 responsibility for up to £0.5m. Negotiating/arranging
                 tenders and contracts on an international level.
                 Creating a new department and leading a team to
                 organise all national/international promotional

events, launches, conferences and exhibitions.
Administration and financial management of leisure
activities, shops, bars, transport and restaurant
facilities. Chairing Executive Committees and
Working Groups.

*Communications/*
*Promotions:* Liaising and negotiating with companies,
institutions and embassies on a world-wide
basis. Advising government bodies/senior
managers on policy and strategy. Presenting
companies and products at national/international
symposia and exhibitions. Training staff on the
implications of event management and
communications skills. Public Speaking. Resolving
conflicts between groups and individuals.
Promoting products/services through various
media, internationally.

## EMPLOYMENT HISTORY

### THE INTERNATIONAL FINANCE GROUP (London)

| | |
|---|---|
| Marketing Communications Manager for Europe | 1989–Present |
| Promotions, Conferences & Exhibitions Manager | 1988–89 |

### EUROPEAN CHAMBER OF COMMERCE (Brussels)

| | |
|---|---|
| Marketing Services Manager | 1987–88 |
| PR + Events Co-ordinator | 1986–87 |

### ABC COMMUNICATIONS SYSTEMS (Paris)

| | |
|---|---|
| Manager | 1985–86 |

### RFJ CIVIL ENGINEERING LTD (Lisbon)

| | |
|---|---|
| International PR Manager | 1983–85 |

## EDUCATION

About to complete the Chartered Institute of Marketing Diploma. BA
Hons French and Spanish with European Economic Studies – Bristol
1981–3

## PERSONAL

Date of birth: 6 June 1960      Status: Single

## The cringe factor

Once you have drafted your CV, read it. Check it for inaccuracies. Is it *truthful*? Does it show you in a positive light? How comfortable do you feel with it? Can you back it up at an interview? It is really quite important that you do not feel *too* comfortable with it – it is after all a *marketing* document and as such must be an exercise in trumpet-blowing – if it makes you cringe just a little with embarrassment then you have probably got it right. If *you* don't tell them how good you are then how will they ever know?

# CHAPTER EIGHT

# *Attacking the Market – or How to Achieve Multiple Interviews*

### In through the window of opportunity

Now you can begin to lay the solid foundations of your job-search road as discussed in Chapter 7. We will look first at the speculative approach, which is displayed in **Figure 6**.

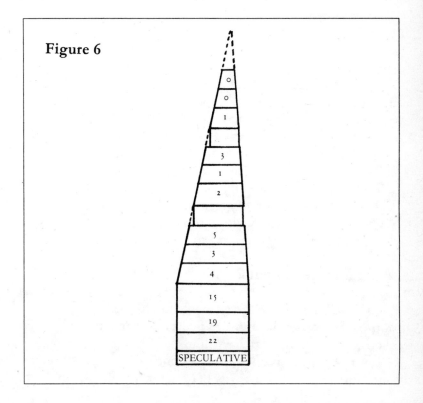

Figure 6

When you see a job advertised, and the 'fit' is such that you are tempted to apply for it, you would naturally be pleased that there is some action you can take, despite the fact that perhaps dozens of other job-seekers will be competing for the position. Your feeling of elation should, however, be tinged with regret – regret that you failed to make a speculative approach to that organization some time previously. Most good advertisements will tell you *why* their *need* exists, eg 'Due to rapid expansion we require...'. Why did you not know that they were expanding? Did you even know that they were in your 'travel to work' area?

The 'window of opportunity' is that period of time between when a need arises and when the employer gets around to doing something about it, eg advertising or briefing an agency. Advertisements do not just suddenly appear. They are preceded by sometimes months of pestering by line managers clamouring for more staff, meetings and discussions between department heads and personnel staff, vacillation on the part of directors – indecision upon indecision! This is why every advertisement is a missed opportunity for at least one job-hunter. Although you may not possess a crystal ball it is possible to exploit the window of opportunity to such an extent that *you* identify the need often before the employer does. A well-timed speculative approach will invariably lead to a job being created for you.

Become pro-active and get in through the window. If your objective is to get a job within the next three months then *the need for that job has almost certainly already arisen.*

## What are the benefits?
Before we look at the 'how?' it is appropriate to deal with the 'why?'. Understanding *why* one should make speculative approaches is useful because as far as job-search techniques go the British in particular are still in the dark ages. The feeling seems to be that it is not quite the done thing to 'go knocking on doors'. Yet, in the 1930s depression this is exactly what

people did – not because it was seen as a sophisticated job-search approach, but through desperation and the knowledge that if there was a job going *someone* was going to get it. Hunger certainly sharpened people's awareness of the *competition* factor in the employment market. That competition factor is no less important today.

### The benefits of speculative approaches, for both yourself and your potential employer

■ **You are *eliminating* the competition – the main barrier in your way.** In the advertised job market you are competing with all those who are looking for a similar type of job, in the same area and at the same time – this may be a handful of people or many hundreds. Here you are competing with no one.

■ **You are displaying *initiative*,** a quality that all employers appreciate and one that is frequently asked for in advertisements. What better way of showing that you have it?

■ **You are being very pro-active and *making things happen*.** This is the only way to maximize your output. Psychologically you will feel that you are really *in control* of your job search and not simply waiting to react to events. Because of this your self-esteem will remain high.

■ **You are saving your potential employer *time* and *money*.** Recruiting even a middle manager by more 'conventional' means can cost many thousands of pounds. The hidden costs are also enormous – the personnel department will be tied up for weeks on end if they are having to advertise. Because your 'application' is not having to be judged along with dozens of others the employer is also able to give *it* more time and consideration.

■ **You are very likely to be reaching the employers before they have firmed up on the 'person profile' to fit the job.** During the window of opportunity few things are decided upon. Once the personnel department is briefed the window is closing – 'age', 'qualifications' and 'experience' can become *fixed* and they may be reluctant to go back on these, *even though their original decisions on these points may have been quite arbitrary*. When the window is open they are much more likely to make the job fit you.

■ **If the combination of your skills and experience is quite rare they are more likely to create a job for you.** How much fruitless searching would they need to do before coming across someone else with your unique range of abilities?

We will now proceed with the 'how?'.

## Narrow your geographical boundary

How you define 'the right job' is of course up to you, but one important factor is likely to be it's *location*. If you have not already done so you must now identify *where* you would like to work. It is no good at all saying 'within reason I don't mind' – this is far too vague. The best way to avoid getting the *wrong* job is not to apply for the wretched thing in the first place, and if the wrong job is one which is in the wrong place then you simply *must* define your geographical boundary clearly.

If you have spent the last 20 years commuting 50 miles every day *now* is an opportunity to discontinue doing it. Initially, then, it would be advisable to concentrate your job-search within a *desirable* travel to work area of, say, 15 miles, and not to make speculative approaches to employers outside this area *for the first two weeks* of your campaign.

Once you have exhausted the possibilities within this area, ie sent out your speculative letters, you can then approach employers within the 15–25 mile travel to work area, and so on. This will of course mean that first interviews for jobs in the 0–15 mile area will be achieved *before* those in the 15–25 mile area. Accordingly, it would be reasonable to assume that job offers nearer to home would accrue before those further distant.

Graphically, your job-search plan would look like Figure 7. In this way your job search will be *systematic*. You are not ignoring employers who are further away, just holding them in abeyance until your speculative approaches to employers nearer to home have been set in train. In a redundancy

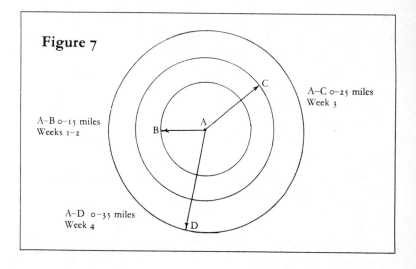

**Figure 7**

A–C 0–25 miles
Week 3

A–B 0–15 miles
Weeks 1–2

A–D 0–35 miles
Week 4

situation particularly, you are in danger of 'panicking' and firing off applications at random – if you apply for a job 50 miles away in the first week of your search, and are offered it – what then? Will it be the *right* job?

## Researching your area

Now that you have defined your area you must research it. Information is food and drink to any job-seeker – without it you cannot function. With the right information you are able to identify employers in your travel to work area who might be interested in what you are selling. Here, we are addressing the final question in the Self Analysis Exercise: 'Who, in my chosen geographical area, might want to buy these skills?'

What you need is information about any *movement* in organizations within which you could and might like to work. Movement means *action*: get in on the action. On pages 12–13 we identified those factors which initiate change within an organization – specifically, change which 'makes the music stop'. You will now be looking for changes which make the music *start*.

As we have already said, 'changes which *remove* career opportunities for some are exactly those which *create* opportunities for others'. If a medium to large sized organization is going through a redundancy exercise in one part of its operation it is not unusual to find that it is recruiting in others. Re-structuring largely means changing the emphasis from one area to another. Don't ignore organizations which *appear* to be going through a bad patch – it is unlikely to be terminal. Takeovers, mergers, new advertising campaigns, acquisitions, new contracts, changes in consumer tastes, government legislation, new appointments to senior positions can all precede job losses – but equally they can be an indicator of new needs.

Read the local/'quality' papers and trade magazines with a fresh eye. Get into the habit of saying 'Alright, XYZ are expanding in this area, can there be a job in it for me?' Planning applications for commercial premises are recorded in the local press and such applications always precede any recruitment. New depots, warehouses or offices cannot run themselves. *Change* means *movement* and we have already seen what movement means.

Strange as it might seem, current or old advertisements can be an excellent source of information. Can you get back copies of your local paper from your library or the paper itself? Who was advertising jobs weeks or months ago that you could have applied for had you been job-hunting then? A lot could have happened in the meantime. Was the position filled? Did they get the right person? Have other needs arisen since? Take a more objective view of *every* advertisement you see, *regardless of the job advertised*. When trawling through the 'sits vac' columns of the newspaper we tend to look for 'job titles' or 'salaries' and if they don't fit what we are looking for we disregard them. In such a way do we miss 'windows of opportunity'. Ask yourself the fundamental questions:

- *Who* are they?
- *Where* are they?

- Is this in my chosen geographical area?
- What do they do?
- What is their need today?
- *Why* do they need this person? (the advertisement will often tell you)
- What *other needs* might they have which are still stuck in the 'window of opportunity'?
- Can they use *me*?

---

**Hazard warning**

- If you identify such a job lead from a current advertisement it is not necessarily in your interests to make a speculative approach immediately. After all, they are up to their eyes in it trying to sort out all the applicants for *that* job – the one you are *not* interested in. Any application by you at this point could well get caught up in that maelstrom – better perhaps to withhold your approach for some days.

---

Readers who feel that age might be against them should be particularly interested in any small to medium sized organizations in their area. Large, well-established companies are likely to be keen on recruiting 'young blood' and may be averse to bringing in anyone above a certain age for all but the most senior or specialized positions. Try aiming for the small 'up and coming' concern which wants to go places and needs experienced people to take it there. It may be reluctant to invest in inexperienced youngsters who 'may be here today and gone tomorrow'. Such organizations realize that there are few 'job-hoppers' over the age of 50.

## Researching the organization

The basic difference between a response to an advertisement and sending a speculative letter is that with the former you would not normally do your company research until you knew that you had achieved an interview. With the latter it is essential that you undertake this research before making the approach. The whole point of doing this is to enable yourself to present some information to the reader of your letter. It will immediately be clear to them that you are not writing simply because you need a job, that you haven't just plucked their name out of the telephone directory and that you have taken the trouble to find out something about them. In effect, it is this which distinguishes the 'sniper's' approach from the 'shotgun' approach (see page 136).

The information you present to them will be such that it has alerted you to believe they might be able to use your skills, ie information about *movement* within their organization. However, such information may be difficult to come across – you cannot *wait* for an advertisement to crop up or for a business article to appear which gives you this information. If all you have to go on is the name and address of a company what do you do then?

If it is a large enough company you could do a lot worse than ring up and request that they send you a copy of their most recent annual report – this is bound to contain some reference to their intentions. Failing that, as they are in your travel to work area why not pay them a visit? If they have some kind of reception area complimentary copies of their literature may be available, and they are almost certain to have some written literature on their products/services.

Your library also can be a good source of the kind of information you want. It is quite surprising how much information on companies is available to the public. The following are some of the better know sources of information available in all good reference libraries. (This is only a *selection* – your librarian will certainly be able to refer you to others.)

## Sources of information
Companies Registration Office
Companies House
Crown Way
Maindy
Cardiff CF4 3UZ

Companies House
55 City Road
London EC1

*Kelly's British Industry and Services in the Common Market*: Published by Kelly's Directories.

*Kelly's Manufacturers and Merchants Directory*: Lists trades or products and suppliers.

*Kompass*: Published by Kompass Publishing in association with the CBI. Lists names and locations of companies plus information on products, services, turnover and management.

*The Times'* 1000 Leading Companies in Britain and Overseas: Published by Times Books. Includes the top 25 trades unions, employers associations and details of companies, their products, chair people and managing directors.

*Who Owns Whom*: Compiled and published by Dun and Bradstreet. Lists subsidiaries and associates of parent companies registered in UK and Eire.

*Key British Enterprises*: Directory of 20,000 companies containing a 'who makes what' index under standard industrial classifications. Also lists directors' names, addresses and telephone numbers.

*Stock Exchange Yearbook*: Financial information on all publicly quoted companies.

*Directory of Directors*: Information on directors of companies with a paid-up capital of £50k or more.

*Careers Guide*: Opportunities in the professions, industry, commerce and the public service (Updated annually).

*Wellings Press Guide* and *Burns Press Directory*: Lists of periodicals and where to order them.

*Dun & Bradstreet*: 5,000 largest UK industrial companies.

Institute of Directors computerized press cuttings search service.

'*Extel*' Cards: Information on quoted and unquoted companies.

*Crawfords City Directory*: banking and finance companies.

## Making the approach

### There are two basic methods of approach:

1. **The 'Shotgun' or 'Blunderbuss' approach.** A *very* unsophisticated method, generally lacking in direction and consisting largely of a massive output of letters fired off in random directions. This 'mailshot' approach can lull you into a false sense of security ('never mind the quality, feel the width').

2. **The 'Sniper's' approach.** With this more sophisticated method one well-aimed shot can get a result. You target specific employers in your declared travel to work area who have given you reason to believe that they might be able to use your skills. Here, your output of letters need not be as great as with the 'shotgun' method but you do need to put more work into each one.

### When should you write?
In terms of time the window of opportunity may be large or small, but is very likely to grow in inverse proportion to the degree of communication and efficiency within the organization itself. Say, for instance, that you identify the need when

the window is open and write to the *personnel department*. What reply could you expect other than a negative one? A letter to them will more often than not result in a reply stating that they have no vacancy – because of course as far as they are aware they haven't. Personnel departments are often the last to know that there is a need – and the larger the organization the more this will be the case.

*Identify your 'target executive'*
Who do you write to? It depends – needs arise in different ways and over different periods of time. Perhaps the appropriate Head of Department, though this depends upon the level of job you might be seeking. Many senior executives have received CVs from executive job-seekers which are so impressive that they are dropped like a hot-plate – either they are perceived as presenting a threat to the reader's job or to their next planned move within the organization. In such circumstances, self-preservation will always come to the fore!

If in doubt go straight to the top – travelling first class really does get results. Your letter may not be read by the MD or Chairman but at the very least it will filter down through the organization and is more likely to arrive on a senior executive's desk than in the personnel department. Whoever receives it will be psychologically under some pressure to do something positive about it.

Always identify your target executive by *name*. There is no point at all in addressing your letter to the Managing Director and then writing 'Dear Sir' on your letter. If the MD is female this approach on its own could ruin all your good work. Either way, a letter without a name lacks the personal touch. If you have been unable to establish the name through library or other resources then simply ring the organization and ask them. You should do this in any case to check that your information is not out of date. You are much more likely, incidentally, to be given the name of senior executives than of anyone in the personnel department.

## Writing the letter

Your letter should be quite brief, no more than one side of A4. You are entering rather dangerous territory: do not be specific about your needs, and least of all about where you see yourself fitting into the organization. Pinning yourself down to what may be quite mythical job titles or objectives would be narrowing the opportunities and making it less likely that a meeting will result. They may have other needs but if they lie outside your *stated* objective they may well think that you wouldn't be interested.

Never ask for a job or mention the word 'vacancy' – you really have to be more subtle than this. There are always alternative ways of saying it which make the whole exercise appear to be less selfish and more employer-orientated. For example, you might enquire if they have an *opening* or, even better, a *need* for someone with your particular talents.

Try to remember that you are not writing because you want a job but because you have got something good to offer them. This shift in emphasis can also be made by your declining to begin the letter with that most selfish of words 'I'. With a little thought you can commence the letter with the words 'you' or 'your' – readers will always be more interested in themselves than in you.

Be sure to emphasize the skills and specific aspects of your experience in which you believe they may be interested. You will of course be including your CV with the letter but don't leave it to do all the work.

All letters should be on white A4 size paper. Do not use the proprietary brands of paper you might normally use for personal correspondence – it looks un-businesslike, unprofessional and does not fit *their* filing system. Use good quality paper and, if at all possible, type all your letters. You are conducting business and all business correspondence is typed. If this is not possible then you are probably running an extremely inefficient campaign but a neatly handwritten letter must suffice.

It is important that the whole tone of your letter conveys enthusiasm and a good self-image. Enthusiasm is infectious – if you have it then they are likely to catch it. Stress your ability to achieve results and show an awareness of the importance of profit and cost-effectiveness. Given that the whole purpose of the letter is to achieve a meeting it is certainly in your interests to *ask* for one. On no account request an 'interview'. The words 'vacancy' and 'interview' can ring all kinds of alarm bells for them which are based upon previous experiences. You do not want to awaken such feelings. Asking for 'a meeting to discuss the possibilities' is less formal and certainly less threatening.

---

### The speculative approach – action checklist

1 Found out something about them?

2 Identified and written to the key decision-maker?

3 Not used the words 'job' or 'vacancy'?

4 Started letter with 'you' or 'your'?

5 Emphasized the skills you can contribute?

6 Not been too specific about *your* needs?

7 Introduced an element of intrigue?

8 Conveyed enthusiasm and good self-image?

9 Asked for a meeting?

10 Given your full telephone number?

11 Closed with 'yours sincerely'?

12 Been sufficiently brief?

## Case study 4

15 Sudbury Square
Liverpool
LP8 4JK

S. Potter Esq.
Chief Representative Europe **2**
Pan Airways
P.A. House
Ruislip
Middlesex
MD1 IL0

15 August 1990

Dear Mr Potter,

**4**  Your airline's reputation and success within the airline
industry has very much impressed me. **1** With the launch of
your Peking–London service beginning in December, and
further routes planned, it has occurred to me that you may
well have an opening for someone with my marketing
**3**  background (in the UK or overseas).

From the enclosed CV you will see that whilst with Sams
Airways I have gained experience in the areas of strategic
marketing, which includes **5** designing **8** successful
marketing plans and promotional strategies for new routes **7**
(one of which was Peking); implementing advertising
**5**  campaigns, **5** evaluating joint ventures and **5** reviewing the
effectiveness of past promotions on sales.

**8**  I am now seeking to broaden my experience within an
airline such as yours, and would **8** welcome the
**6**  prospect of working in the more frontline areas such as
product and sales management development. It is also likely
that my skills could **5** contribute greatly to your plans for
developing new routes.

Should you be interested in discussing the possibilities I
would be **9** very pleased to come and see you. I am
available during the day **10** on 042 6843 or in the evenings
on 042 8943.

**12**

**11**  Yours sincerely,

Mark Clark

Mark's letter satisfies all of the requirements on the action checklist. Notice how the CV is introduced quite early in the letter – 'From the enclosed CV you will see . . .' This encourages the reader to look at the CV and if you tell people that they *will* see something then they are more inclined to see it. You might otherwise be tempted to leave any reference to your CV until the end of the letter eg 'I enclose my CV for your information'. This is not really strong enough and fails to give the CV the emphasis it deserves.

Notice also that the writer declines to say *why* he is looking for a job other than to state that he is seeking to broaden his experience. *Why* you are in the job market is not relevant at this stage and this is something to discuss at the meeting.

A speculative approach such as this will frequently result in a reply stating that although the employers do not have a vacancy they would be willing to meet with you to discuss the possibilities. You might be forgiven for thinking 'Well, if they don't have a job there's not a lot of point in seeing them'. This would be a grave error on your part. Go to the meeting but don't believe that they have nothing for you. It is more likely that they have something in mind but are not prepared to share it with you until they have seen you.

Even if you receive a negative reply you have at least opened up a line of communication. You can keep it going by telephoning them, thanking them for taking the trouble to reply to your letter and asking them if they are aware of who else might be able to use your skills. They are on the inside and may have important information to which you are not privy. Such information is unlikely to be volunteered unless you ask for it.

---

**Hazard warning**

■ In ending your speculative letter you may be tempted to adopt a more 'aggressive' approach by saying 'I will telephone you next Thursday to discuss the possibilities further'. This 'hard sell' approach is often recommended but there is little evidence to suggest that it gets results. In fact, it is more likely to receive very short shrift indeed – if they have been impressed by your letter such an ending can ruin all the good work. On the whole people do not take kindly to being threatened with a phone call and are more than likely to instruct their secretary to 'close the door on you' when you telephone.

---

## *How to develop your personal contacts*

Achieving interviews through personal contacts represents a potentially huge part of your market and one that you ignore at your peril. 'Networking', as it is more popularly known (and we shall see why in a moment) is essential whether you are seeking the right job while already employed or unemployed. The problem with being unemployed in this respect is that you are often physically removed from the very people who could be of most benefit. Anyone going through the trauma of enforced redundancy will be all too familiar with the mental stress induced by such a situation. Such stress is not at all conducive to mounting a positive and pro-active job-search campaign.

As a result, the one aspect of the job search to suffer most is invariably that of personal networking. This is hardly surprising. The last thing we are inclined to do, at least in those quite crucial early days, is to shout from the roof-tops that we have no means of earning a living. Indeed, the natural inclination is to do the exact opposite and tell no one except those closest to us (and not always them).

The result is that those very people who could be of the greatest assistance to us remain impotent and inactive, because as far as they are concerned nothing has changed and we are still in gainful employment. This is a bit like a general omitting to tell his troops that there is a war on.

At first sight, the whole idea of networking does tend to conjure up a rather unattractive picture of waylaying former colleagues on street corners as *they* come home from work. It need not be like that. In fact it is essential that one doesn't *pester* friends or acquaintances. It can be as difficult for them to adjust to your change of circumstances as it is for you. They may even begin to feel guilty if they are in work and you are not. After a while they may disappear over the horizon when they see you coming.

For these reasons your networking must be done carefully and tactfully. If you go about it in any other way you will place your contacts in invidious positions, alienate them and even ruin what may have been long-standing friendships. Take it one step at a time:

## Step 1
Compile a list of *all* your personal contacts, regardless of whether you believe they can be of any use to you. Include:

- Friends
- Acquaintances
- Colleagues
- Ex-colleagues
- Neighbours
- Customers, ex-customers, clients, suppliers
- Relations

For this part of the exercise a contact is *anyone* you know. Do not be selective. Do no 'prioritize' your contacts in terms of their potential 'usefulness' – this is the biggest mistake a job-seeker can make at this stage. Compiling the list does not commit you to anything and you will not necessarily be contacting them all but if you fail to make the list exhaustive you are in danger of making pre-emptive decisions and 'throwing the baby out with the bath water'.

## Step 2
*Now* you can prioritize your list. This doesn't mean taking names off the list but putting them in some semblance of order. Identify and separate out those on the list who, to the best of your knowledge, are *in a working environment*, regardless of what that environment is. The reason for this is that such people are likely (though not always) to be more 'contact rich' than those not in work. You now have two lists.

## Step 3
Initially, you may wish to use your first list (those in work) for this stage – it will depend largely on the extent of each list. Ask yourself the fundamental question 'Are all these people aware that I am in the job market?' If they are not you must make them aware. This can be done in an infinite number of ways but it does mean that you will have to devise a means of initiating contact.

If they are people you had dealings with on a regular basis at work ie customers, clients or suppliers then this should not be too difficult – after all it is courteous to inform them that you will no longer be available to tend to their needs. In most of these situations the information you give should go no further than this. Asking them for anything at this stage may be most inappropriate. Your aim here is to acquaint them with the position and thereby lay the groundwork for a subsequent follow-up. You are facilitating a situation for the future. This may sound devious and it is, a little, but this is just as much to protect your contacts as it is to get you a result.

## Step 4
The situation you aim to facilitate is one whereby your contacts can act as your eyes and ears. They can only do this effectively if you give them an indication of what they should

be seeing and hearing. This means letting them know what you have done and what you would like to do. Try the following exercise. Think of someone you know well and who has a job outside your line of work. How much do you know about what they actually do? Make a list. What are their responsibilities? What functions do they perform? (be specific). What professional skills do they employ on a day to day basis? What is their status in relation to their colleagues? What have they achieved? If your list does not get much beyond an employer's name and a job title then you would be of little use to them if they suddenly found themselves in the job market.

Now ask yourself how much they really know about you. The odds are that they wouldn't get much further than you did. For them to be of any use to you at all you must now furnish them with this information, and what better way of doing it than by giving them a copy of your CV? Don't make the mistake of pinning them in a corner of the bar and regaling them with your life story. They will not be in any way affronted to receive a copy of your CV, as long as you make it clear that you do *not* expect them to find you a job. On the contrary, they will probably be keen to help and feel flattered to be asked, particularly if you ask for their comments on your CV and say that you would welcome any suggestions on how it might be improved.

## Step 5

Having given them a copy of your CV give them your permission to pass it on to *their contacts*. If you do not give them your express permission to do this they will be most unlikely to do it, not through any disinclination on their part but because they will see your CV as being a very personal document. Should you fail to take this step your 'networking' will not in fact take place for the CV will remain stuck at the first point of contact. Networking, as the term implies, is not all about 'who you know', but also, and more importantly, about who *they* know. To be effective your CV must travel on down through the network – it will only do so if you give it that initial impetus.

It may take a number of weeks for your network to build up so you must set it in train right from the beginning. The good news is that, unlike any other part of your market, this is the only job-search route where your sources of information actually *multiply* as you go along – but only, of course, if you follow the right steps.

## Handling the job lead

Your contacts are useful, not only in introducing you to their contacts, but in drawing your attention to other leads which will result in your making some kind of approach. With the best will in the world, and however diligent your job search, it is simply not possible for you to identify every job lead that may arise. A most suitable job may be advertised today, but not in any newspaper you read. There is a chance that one of your contacts may see it, but of course it won't register if they are unaware that you have a need.

Your contacts will not always get it right – you will no doubt be given leads which are way off beam, so be careful how you handle this. Accept all leads graciously, even if you know them to be of little use to you. If your reaction is dismissive and you say 'no, that's no good to me' you will be transmitting unfavourable signals. They are likely to feel rejected and will almost certainly think twice before offering another lead which may be *the* one.

As a result of networking you will almost certainly be invited to informal meetings with people you don't personally know. Treat these referrals with some sensitivity. You may initially be seen as a threat, and in seeing you they may only be doing so as a favour to a mutual friend. These contact meetings are all about information gathering, so go with a clear idea of your objectives in terms of what you want to find out. Keep an open mind on what you believe they might be able to do for you. Either they have a need for someone with your skills or they know someone who might. Again, give them permission to pass on your CV to their contacts – they may not do so unless you give them the green light.

When networking it is essential that you do not give your contacts the impression that you are asking them for a job or to find you a job. You will be contacting people you know, however vaguely you know them, and asking them for a job may be something that is not within their gift – this may embarrass or antagonize them. The line to take is that you are merely seeking *advice* – on the direction you might take, on local employment opportunities, on a particular sector of the job market, on potential target employers or on your CV.

## The importance of the follow-up letter

All referral meetings, ie meetings with someone you did not previously know and arranged by someone you did know, must be followed up by letter – even if the meeting itself appeared to come to nothing. Failure to 'follow through' and keep open lines of communication is perhaps the most common error committed by job-hunters – an error which continually occurs throughout the four market sectors. If you fail to follow through *you will become history* in the minds of your contacts. If they hear nothing further from you they will assume that you have achieved your objective and are no longer job-hunting. You simply cannot allow the trail to go cold.

Quite apart from this these contacts have given you their time – a valuable commodity as we have already seen. It is only courteous to write and thank them. This will make them feel appreciated (which they are), act as a memory jogger, and is also an opportunity for you to clarify any point which you feel needs to be clarified. When was the last time you received a note of thanks from someone? Your answer, unfortunately, is likely to be 'Never'. This is precisely why it is so important for you to do it – time and time again successful job search has been *proved* to be all about doing the unexpected, the unusual –

doing all those things that others would not dream of doing. So often such actions are not earth-shattering in their significance, they are simply the by-products of common sense and common courtesy – neither of which are at all common.

## Using executive search/selection agencies

The term 'job agency' is a somewhat generic term which can be used to describe a wide (and confusing) range of organizations performing specific functions on behalf of their clients (employers). Some will only take on the advertising function and not become involved in the screening of applicants. Others will be very closely involved with their clients to the extent that they advise on the 'person specification', ie tell the clients what kind of person they should be seeking and then find them. They will screen carefully and interview thoroughly their selected candidates – only then will the successful candidate(s) be recommended for interview by the client company.

The first thing to remember is that no agency is interested in finding you a job. This is not their role in life (in fact, *no one* can find you a job, except you. The most any third party can do is get you an interview). Agencies are paid by their client to take on one or more of the roles normally performed by in-house personnel specialists. Their first priority is to *maintain their client base* because this is where their income lies.

This does not necessarily mean that your interests and the interests of their clients are mutually exclusive – if they are professional they will treat both parties in a professional manner. However, it does mean that they are not particularly interested in whether *the job* is right *for you* in terms of your career development. They would be most unlikely to persuade you to turn down a job offer achieved through their services because they felt that it wasn't right for you.

You can kick up a lot of dust by running around from one agency to another and be lulled into a false sense of security by the reassuring noises made by them. The first step is to be selective and identify those agencies which:

- Specialize in the type of employment of interest to you
- Are located within your identified job-search area
- Specialize in the type of salary range you require

This information can be found in *Executive Grapevine* (Oxford University Press), available in most reference libraries.

You can then either telephone the agency and ask them how they would like you to proceed or send them a copy of your CV with a *detailed* letter (not simply a covering letter) highlighting what you see as your 'unique selling points', indicating *what* type of job you are seeking, *where* you would prefer to work geographically and the salary *range* you are prepared to consider. You may then be contacted by telephone and asked to go and see them or you may not be contacted at all. If it is the latter follow up after seven working days and ask if they have received your letter and whether they feel that a meeting would be appropriate.

A good agency will, if preparing you for a meeting with their client, give you a briefing on their needs and a preliminary interview – which, incidentally, may be even more rigorous than that subsequently given by that client. The agency has its reputation to consider and will not put you forward if it feels that you lack credibility.

Agencies advertising a vacancy on behalf of their client will tend not to disclose the identity of that client. When applying either give them a list of employers to whom you do not wish your CV to be sent or instruct the agency not to despatch your CV without your approval.

### Case study 5
Trevor was a senior manager in his late thirties and seeking a new job, his previous position having been made redundant.

He had prepared an excellent two-page CV and, by prior arrangement, took it with him to an agency. They were very optimistic and inferred that 'fixing him up with a job' was not going to be a problem. However, they were not happy with his CV and said it that it did not give enough information – in order to do anything for him they would have to 're-vamp' it a little. The conversation moved on and much was discussed – his family background, most recent and previous salaries, his reasons for leaving previous positions and his hopes for the future. The meeting was enjoyable and ended with them requesting that he 'leave it with them'.

Trevor was very encouraged by this and, as other agencies were making similar noises, became increasingly reluctant to attack the remainder of the market. He therefore made no speculative approaches and did not activate his network of personal contacts. A few days later he was astonished to receive from the agency a copy of his 'new CV' accompanied by a letter informing him that they had already despatched this CV to a number of their 'blue chip' clients.

The new CV was now nine pages in length and divulged much of the information that he had revealed 'in confidence' at the meeting but omitted to put on his original CV: the fact that he had been recently divorced, that he had left a previous job (15 years previous) because of a personality clash with a colleague and all the reasons for his various career moves. In addition, all his previous salaries were listed. In fact, his whole life was bare on nine pages of A4.

Trevor could have just put this down to experience but, disastrously, some of the companies the CV had been sent to were key organizations in his field that he had previously decided to approach on his own behalf.

There are obviously lessons to be learnt from Trevor's experience:

■ Many agencies will not be prepared to submit your CV to their clients until they have rearranged it to fit their standard format. This is both a means of justifying their fee to the client company and of maintaining a standard format for their data base. Do not allow them to despatch your CV until you have vetted it yourself and given them the go-ahead

- If there are employers you do not want them to approach you must make this clear to them
- Once you have 'activated' your agencies you simply must get on with the rest of your job-search campaign. In some cases you will walk into an agency at exactly the right time, ie when they have a vacancy on their desk which is suitable for you. More often than not, however, they will have nothing and, despite their optimism (it is not in their interests for you to visit other agencies) you will be history as soon as you leave
- Treat all meetings with agencies as professionally as you would a job interview. They are naturally interested in assessing your 'marketability' which includes not just your expertise and 'track record' but your ability to be interviewed

## The advertised vacancy

The advertised job market is not an aspect of the market you can afford to ignore, but to achieve success through this route requires you to sell yourself better than most at the application stage, and better than anyone else at the interview. You are now in direct competition with others so great care must be taken to avoid the pitfalls which lead to rejection.

The application letter 'personalizes' your CV and tailors it to specific jobs. It does this by displaying attributes such as enthusiasm, initiative, positive thinking and (carefully) humour.

But just as letters can display personality/character attributes they can also, and frequently do, act as an advertisement for character *defects*. Perhaps the most common criticism to be levelled at application letters is that they are too self-effacing, even subservient, and often project an extremely poor *self-image*. This is hardly surprising since many job-hunters are seeking work from a position of unemployment or impending redundancy – at which times the self-image is unlikely to be good – and how we feel about ourselves is reflected in how we act and in what we say.

## Case study 6

---

### INDUSTRIAL ENGINEERING MANAGER c £30K

We are undertaking a major expansion and investment programme – automating our manufacturing facilities to provide a range of products for the Electronics Industry. An enthusiastic Industrial Engineering Manager is to be appointed to assume responsibility for this project and head up a team providing a vital interface between engineering and manufacturing. Responsibilities will also include the management of site services and the works engineer will report directly.

Applicants must have experience in the electronics industry, will preferably be graduates and are likely to be within the age range 35–45. Experience of PCB and Mechanical Assembly in the automation of the manufacturing process and in the introduction of new products in the fields of electronics or instrumentation are essential requirements. Previous site management experience would be useful. Location – South Coast.

Please send full details to: The Managing Director
CW Electronics
Sherwood House
London W1A 2BE

---

As advertisements go, this one is better than average. The employer begins by giving some background to the vacancy (which, remember, should be of great interest to speculative applicants, see page 132) and proceeds to give a 'shopping list' of needs. It is quite likely that they would be willing to compromise on the age and qualification requirement provided the applicant has those requirements preceded by the word 'must'. There are indicators such as 'preferred' and 'likely' which tell us those factors on which they might be prepared to negotiate.

Bill Thompson is going to apply for this job. He is aged 50, has no degree and is still working although his present job is due to become redundant. He is deserving of an interview because he could do the job well and has many of the skills the employer is seeking. Unfortunately, the employer is not aware of this and Bill has chosen to highlight other things in his letter – things which will encourage the reader to say 'no thank you'.

Bill's letter (see page 154) is typical of those received by employers every day. In fact, although it contains many of the cardinal errors, it is still better than many applicants' letters. He will not get an interview because he has failed to overcome the pitfalls.

### The major faults of Bill's letter

1. **His letter is hand-written.** As we have already said, job-hunting is a business – business correspondence is typed.

2. **He has not bothered to find out the *name* of the person he is writing to.** Unless a name is given in the advertisement, *always* ring up the appropriate department and elicit the name and initials of the person you are going to write to.

3. **He has left out both his post-code and telephone number.**

4. **He does not say *which* job he is applying for.** The company may currently be advertising several different positions through several different media.

5. **He says he 'wishes' to apply.** Employers don't want 'wishers', and in any case he *is* applying.

64 Havant Drive
Shedfield
Sussex

The Managing Director
CW Electronics
Sherwood House
London W1A 2BE

1st April 1991

Dear Sir,

I am interested in your advertisement and wish to apply.

I have spent a lifetime in manufacturing and for the past ten years have been the Senior Production Engineer in one of the leading electronics companies in the UK. However, due to excessively high interest rates, investment has been cut back and I have now been made redundant.

I am interested in this position because it would give me the opportunity to utilize my experience and increase my level of responsibility. Although I am over the age limit for this position, I still feel that I can make a useful contribution to your organization.

I enclose my CV and hope to hear from you in the near future.

Yours faithfully,

Bill Thompson.

W. E. THOMPSON

6. **Bill may feel that 'spending a lifetime' in manufacturing is a good way of saying 'look how experienced I am'.** Unfortunately, the reader is more likely to interpret this as 'look how *old* I am'.

7. **He says *he* has been made redundant.** Remember, *jobs* get made redundant, not *people*. If you are job-hunting from a position of redundancy be very careful about how you get this across. *Never* give excuses (as Bill does) for such a position.

8. **Bill fails to make clear exactly what it is that he is selling.** 'I am interested . . . increase my level of responsibility' puts the emphasis on what *they* can do for *him*, rather than on what *he* can contribute. Although the advertisement made clear what the needs are, no attempt has been made to match those needs.

9. **'Although I am over the age limit' is a classic example of giving reasons why an employer *shouldn't* see you.** Any natural inclination to be accommodating and furnish the recipient with all the facts must be kept in check.

10. **'Hope to hear from you' doesn't sound very hopeful at all** – employers don't want 'hopers' any more than they want 'wishers'. This ending adds to the lack of enthusiasm which permeates Bill's letter. It is particularly damaging here since enthusiasm is one of the qualities asked for in the advertisement.

11. **Even though he is still on the payroll of his present employer, Bill states directly that he soon won't be.** Jobs do not become redundant until the last day of the termination of contract (normally 90 days after notice has been given). Remember, it is far easier to get a job while you still have one.

Clearly, even if Bill has an excellent CV (which is unlikely as sub-standard CVs typically accompany poor letters) he has a lot of work to do to bring his letter up to scratch. The following is an example of how he could have improved upon it.

64 Havant Drive
Shedfield
Sussex
SD9 4BX

A L Howard
Managing Director
CW Electronics
Sherwood House
London W1A 2BE

2 April 1991

Dear Mrs Howard,

*Industrial Engineering Manager*

Your advertisement for the above position very much interests me and I
enclose my CV from which you will see that my experience closely
matches your requirements.

In my present position I have direct responsibility for the application of
automation and new technology in the production and engineering office
environments. This includes leading the project teams for the successful
development of advanced robotic assembly cells which are now running
effectively.

As major benefits can also be achieved by using advanced technologies
in the design and manufacturing engineering offices I took the lead in
introducing a network of engineering stations, and a CAD system, into
the departments involved in these processes. The opportunities offered by
these technologies to improve the design and manufacturing interface,
and to develop a simpler fully integrated 'paperless' environment were
seized and became a major contributor towards progressive staff
reductions of 50%.

Designing and equipping a completely new facility for the volume
production of complex PCB assemblies has also been part of my remit.
This included the selection of state of the art automated assembly,
materials movement and test systems which led to the development of
several innovative production methods.

Consolidating my experience of new technologies in the engineering/
electronics fields is now my aim and the position advertised is exactly
what I am seeking. I would be delighted to discuss the possibilities at an
interview and can be contacted on 0463 911 (day) or 0463 223
(evenings).

Your sincerely,

W E Thompson

It is hard to believe that the revised letter is from the same person who concocted the first one. Which Mr Thompson would *you* interview? The second letter is much more likely to achieve an interview because:

- Bill pays attention to detail by including his postcode and has had the initiative to find out the name of the Managing Director
- The letter is well-presented, easy to read and contains no errors
- Although he is over the age limit, has no degree and his present job is due to become redundant, he is not wearing his heart on his sleeve. He *knows* he can do this job and is saying so with confidence
- Unlike many of his competitors for the job he is not 'wishing' and 'hoping'. There is conviction in his letter
- He has not fallen into the trap of expecting his CV to do all the work for him. He is highlighting those aspects of his career that appear to be relevant to the job. He will of course take the precaution of stapling his letter to the CV to prevent them from becoming separated
- He is encouraging the reader to look at his CV – 'you will see' – and saying that he has got what they are looking for – 'my experience closely matches your requirements'
- He is not 'redundant' but seeking to 'consolidate my experience'
- He uses words which send the right signals eg 'leading', 'successful', 'benefits', 'opportunities', 'improve', 'seized', 'contributor', 'progressive'
- He clearly gives the impression that he is a person who can *get results*
- He is clearly aware that a business exists to make a profit and reduce overheads – 'staff reductions of 50%'

- He has *intrigued* the reader. Can the Managing Director afford *not* to find out about those 'innovative production methods'?
- There is no humility in the letter. Even though it may go against his natural inclination, he knows that if ever he is going to blow his own trumpet this is the time to do it. It is of course important not to overdo it: there are great rewards to be had from heaping praise on others but this is used to best effect at the interview
- He remembers to ask for the interview and ensures that his full telephone numbers follow it up. When the letter is being read, the reader's telephone is usually but a few tantalizing centimetres away – make them pick it up

In this case study we have seen two quite different responses to the same advertisement. 'Both' applicants were in exactly the same position, ie not highly qualified academically, over the age limit stipulated in the advertisement and facing redundancy. They had quite different attitudes to their predicament, reflected in the quality of their respective letters.

The 'first' applicant was already defeated. Because he saw himself as a failure he *was* a failure – he could only see his situation as it was and no further. He believed he was applying for a *job* and if he had any objective at all it was probably simply to write a letter – any letter.

The 'second' applicant had *vision*. He was not dwelling on the situation as it was but concentrating on *how it was going to be in the future*. He was a success because he *saw* himself as a success. He understood that although his ultimate goal was to get the job offer his immediate objective was to secure an interview.

When you have drafted a letter in response to an advertisement, check it for quality by using the following action checklist.

---

**Responding to an advertised vacancy – action checklist**

■ Typed. A4 good quality paper. No errors?
■ Asked for a job description?
■ Written to a name?
■ Specified clearly the job for which you are seeking interview?
■ Minimized use of the word 'I'?
■ No 'wishing' or 'hoping'?
■ Used positive words like 'achieve', 'success' 'contribute'?
■ Studied the advertisement – identified *their* needs?
■ Shown how you could meet those needs?
■ Conveyed enthusiasm. Good self-image?
■ Quantified where appropriate?
■ Accentuated the positive, eliminated the negative?
■ Shown that you can get results?
■ Intrigued the reader?
■ Paid attention to detail?
■ Asked for the interview?
■ Given your full telephone number?
■ Attached your letter to the CV?
■ Letter is the *best* example of the work you are capable of producing?

---

## Application forms – some hazards to avoid

Application forms are enough to make even the most stalwart of job-hunters burst into tears. The average application form is very average indeed. The receipt of a form after you have already sent a CV and application letter is surely designed to induce apoplexy. It is also hard to understand why one is obliged to shoe-horn a lengthy response into a box the size of a toe nail when on the very next page an acre of space is provided to explain why one has never (until now) suffered from Dysthymia. Having said that, there really is no alternative but to fill the wretched thing in and give it the respect it does not deserve.

Much of an application form requests factual information, which is not normally a problem, but there are certain areas which demand some thought before putting pen to paper.

When requesting the required form (either by telephone or letter) ask if there is a job specification they can send you. There often is but this additional information about the job is not always volunteered. On receipt of the application form always get it photocopied. Put the original in a safe place and do not touch it until you have drafted all your comments onto the copy and are happy with the results. Nothing looks more slipshod and unprofessional than poor layout and untidy corrections. Make your mistakes on the copy, which you will keep for your own records. Neat presentation here is just as important as it is with letters and CVs.

Take careful notice of any instructions on how to complete the form eg 'black ink', 'block letters' or 'typed'. (Beware – this instruction is sometimes to be found at the end of the form!) If there are no instructions then always print in black ink or type. Obey all instructions and do not leave blank spaces. Whenever a particular section is not relevant to your circumstances put N/A for 'Not Applicable'.

It is perfectly in order for you to send a CV with the form but on no account make it part of your application, ie never complete a section of the form by writing 'see attached CV'. Employers tend to find this extremely irritating.

As we have already said, you should not volunteer your salary if applying in any other way but by application form. Thankfully, employers are becoming increasingly aware of the iniquitous nature of such questions and are omitting them from their forms. However, the practice is still quite common. You can of course leave it blank but this could stop you from getting the interview. If you choose to disclose this information, think in terms of TRP (see page 187). If they ask what salary you are seeking put either 'negotiable' or 'tbd' for 'to be discussed'.

| NATIONAL NEWSPAPER ADVERTISEMENTS: WHERE AND WHEN TO FIND THEM | | | | | | | |
|---|---|---|---|---|---|---|---|
| *Sector* | *Mon.* | *Tues.* | *Wed.* | *Thurs.* | *Fri.* | *Sat.* | *Sun.* |
| *Accountancy* | | Indep. | | Times | | | |
| *Building/ Construction* | | D.Expr. | D.Mail | | D.Mail | | |
| *Computing* | Indep. | Times | | Guard. | | | |
| *Creative/ Media* | Guard. | | Times Indep. D.Tel. D.Expr. | D.Mail | Indep. | Guard. | |
| *Education* | Times D.Tel. | Guard. | | Indep. | | | |
| *Engineering/ Technology* | Indep. | D.Tel | D.Mail | Times Guard. D.Expr. | | | |
| *Finance* | | Indep. D.Tel. | D.Mail | Times Guard. | | | |
| *General* | | | | Indep. D.Tel. Guard. D.Expr. Times | | Guard. | Observer Sun.Tel. Sun.Times Sun.Corr. |
| *Legal* | | Times | | Times | Indep. Guard. | | |
| *Print* | | D.Expr. | D.Mail | | D.Mail | | |
| *Public* | D.Tel. D.Mail | Times | Guard. | Indep. D.Expr. | | | |
| *Sales & Marketing* | Guard. | | Times Indep. D.Tel. D.Expr. | D.Mail | Indep. | Guard. | |
| *Secretarial* | Times Guard. | Indep. D.Expr. D.Mail | Times | Times Indep. | | Guard. | |

Make sure that you give positive reasons for leaving previous jobs. If your current job is due to become redundant but the termination date has not been reached then put 'still employed'. It is worth remembering that if you secure alternative employment while still under notice of redundancy you have done so *before* your job became redundant. Therefore, when it *did* become redundant it was not your job. If your termination date has passed and you are unemployed then 'company restructuring' or 'opportunity to broaden experience' are suitable reasons for leaving. Fortunately, redundancy does indeed present you with an opportunity to do just that.

A section of the form which is abused more than any other is normally to be found under the heading 'state your reasons for applying for this position' or, more mysteriously, 'give any other information in support of your application'. This provokes a half-hearted response from most applicants and, alarmingly, is often left blank altogether. The contents of this section should be those that would have gone in your application letter had you been allowed to submit one. The reason it is often left blank is not difficult to understand. Just as many job-hunters will submit a poor application letter (expecting the CV to do all the work for them) they will likewise expect the rest of the application form (the CV equivalent) to be enough to do the job. It isn't. The 'other information' category is your opportunity to give them all the reasons why they *must* see you.

Keep your completed copy in a safe place. You will be at a distinct disadvantage when you are called for an interview if you have no recollection of what you said on your form. *They* will have it in front of them on the day and may refer to it during the interview.

Don't just fold the form up and despatch it in a small envelope – use an A4 envelope and enclose a *covering letter* – yet again a businesslike and courteous approach. Your letter should say something along the following lines:

'Dear Mr [Identify your target executive]

Thank you for forwarding the application form for the above position which I now return completed as requested.

The Job Description was most interesting and for your additional information I enclose my CV which shows the relevance of my experience.

I would be very pleased to discuss the possibilities with you at an interview and can be contacted on 045 68904.

Yours sincerely,

John Brown

# CHAPTER NINE

## Managing the Interview – or How to Achieve Multiple Job Offers

### Preparing for the meeting

The job-search road has now led to the interview. However, as the word 'interview' is far too close to 'inquisition' for comfort we shall, from now on, use the word 'meeting'. This is not just a matter of semantics or seeking to be different – it is a means of restoring the relationship between employer and potential employee to its rightful balance. Traditionally it has been assumed, by both parties, that such meetings must take on an inquisitorial air – *they* ask the questions and you provide the answers. It need not be like that. Unfortunately, it *is* like that for many job-seekers who are satisfied for it to be so and who go unprepared. It will undoubtedly turn into an inquisition if you choose to let it. To get a good result you must go with the right *attitude* and the right attitude is one which is formed through an understanding that the aim of the meeting is for both parties to establish whether or not *they can fulfil each other's needs*. No more, no less.

These meetings can take on many forms: personal contact meetings which may be quite informal (though no less 'dangerous'); more formal affairs where the needs are quite strictly defined; and meetings as a result of speculative approaches where the needs have not been declared by the employer. You will need to adjust your approach to meet each situation as it arises. However, the basic ground rules remain the same regardless of the nature of the meeting.

Much has been written about 'interviews' and how to handle them and it is not the purpose of this chapter to cover areas which are already well-documented elsewhere. We have seen throughout this book that successful career planning and job search is all about:

- Planning and preparation
- Having the initiative to take certain actions which are outside 'the norm' and which, because of this, *get you noticed*

Getting a result from a meeting is no different. As our model we will assume that this particular meeting has been achieved as a result of an application for an advertised position. This will ensure that the ground rules are covered and you will simply need to adapt them to fit other circumstances. We will begin by discussing the actions you should be taking *before* attending the meeting for, make no mistake, this is where the battle is either won or lost.

On receipt of a letter asking you to attend a meeting read it carefully. Does it tell you all you need to know? It is very rare for them to give you all the information you require. Consider the following:

- Have they made it clear *who* your meeting will be with? They may give you the name of someone to contact on arrival but this may not be the person you will be seeing. Far too many people go to these meetings with no idea who their meeting will be with. This is ludicrous – no professional businessperson would attend a meeting in such circumstances. Remember, the job search *is* business. It can throw you mentally off balance to be confronted by a panel of people when you were expecting to be dealing with just one person. If you know beforehand who they are and their positions in the organization then their names will be locked into your memory and you can address them by name at the meeting

- They will always of course tell you what time the meeting is due to start, but rarely will they inform you of the time it is due to finish. You need this information for two reasons. Firstly, you are busy and have other appointments to keep (if you don't then you must re-read Chapter 7). Secondly, because you are going there to sell your skills you need to know how long you have got to make the sale – if they have only given you an hour you cannot afford to be leisurely about it. You cannot prepare effectively without knowing how much time they have allotted

- Have they provided you with any information on their organization? We will see later the importance of doing some homework on the company but this doesn't have to be a 'cloak and dagger' exercise. The best source is the organization itself. Ring them up and ask if they can send any material. This is a 'no lose' question for you – if they say 'no' then at least you have had the initiative to ask for it and you can still do your homework through other means. If they say 'yes' then you may get some material that your competitors will not have. Accept gratefully anything they offer to send you (Annual Report, brochures, sales literature, 'in-house' magazine etc) – *what* you get is not important, *asking the question* is

Even if they have furnished you with all of the above information you will still need to telephone them. Why? To *confirm that you will be attending*. Very few of your competitors will bother to do this and it is extremely un-businesslike. This telephone call is not an 'optional extra', it is *essential* if you want to stand out from the crowd. Your aim is to 'make a friend at Court' before you get to the meeting. The message will invariably get back to those who matter that *this* candidate has already shown courtesy, initiative and enthusiasm.

---

### Hazard warning

■ When telephoning, try to be sensitive to what is happening at the other end. It is not difficult to sense when they are extremely busy, in which case the last thing they want is someone on the end of the line asking a string of questions – be prepared simply to confirm that you will be attending and leave it at that. It is just as easy to make an enemy as it is to make a friend. An additional hazard is that you never know who will take the call. It is possible that you could end up being 'interviewed' over the phone – though this should only be a hazard if you are unprepared for it and if your telephone skills are not very sophisticated.

---

## Follow up

Even though you have confirmed verbally that you will be attending, follow it up with a letter of confirmation. Telephone calls are transient, letters are not. If your telephone call does not reach the ears of those who matter your letter will reach their eyes. Again, this is a businesslike action to take.

Notice, incidentally, that none of the above actions are likely to have any bearing whatsoever on your ability to do the job, but they are an indication of your 'interpersonal skills'. You may be able to do the job standing on your head but if they don't like you then you will not be given the opportunity of showing them.

## Anticipating their questions

Your written application was designed by you to provoke questions. But what should those questions be and do you have the answers? *Write down* the questions you think may be asked and then *write down* and *edit* the answers you might give. Remember them. Make sure they contain positives and not negatives. Be relevant and future-orientated. Ensure that your responses provoke further questions which will act as an enabling vehicle for you to get across more selling points. Concentrate on *their* needs – initially least they will not be very interested in what they can do for you.

Know your weaknesses because you must be able to defend them in a positive way – you must be able to counter any possible 'objections to the sale'. Not all of the questions you anticipate will arise but no matter, this is an excellent way of getting to know your own product.

## Preparing your questions

Prepare written questions to ask them. The meeting is a two-way street. Towards the end of the interview they will always give you an opportunity to ask something. It is no good at all responding by saying 'I don't have any questions at this stage, you have covered all the points very thoroughly'. Such a response will almost guarantee that there won't be a second stage. This is normally the point during the meeting when your competitors will stop selling. This is a tremendous opportunity to impress and you must carry on selling.

Ask pertinent questions about the job itself and the company ie continue showing an interest in what you can *contribute*. If you ask questions about holidays, salary and various perks they will get the impression that you are only interested in what they can do for you. Don't leave all this to chance, you will undoubtedly think of questions to ask during the meeting but have a reserve list written down on a piece of card and don't be afraid to produce it at the appropriate point – this presents them with *physical evidence* that you have given it some thought and taken the trouble to prepare. They cannot fail to be impressed.

Always prepare more questions than you will actually ask. If you only go armed with three questions they will probably be answered during the course of the meeting and then you will really have to think on your feet. You may wish to ask one or more of the following questions, bearing in mind that all interview situations are unique and you may need to alter them accordingly.

## Questions to ask at an interview

■ **How do you see the company developing over the next five years?.** This is showing an interest in *them*. If they have already revealed the 'game plan' then of course don't ask it. You may, however, wish to ask a question about that plan. Be careful not to ask this question of someone who may not be qualified to answer it. You may be initially meeting someone quite junior in the organization in which case you don't want to embarrass them. Better to ask such a person how long they have been in the company and if they enjoy it – people will generally warm to you if you show an interest in them.

■ **How has this vacancy arisen?** If it is a new position then presumably they will have explained the reason for the need. But what if you are replacing someone? You have a right to know what has happened to your predecessor. Have they left the company? Why? Have they been promoted? To what position? How long were they in this job *before* being promoted? These questions are *not* impertinent: if they have been waxing lyrical about your prospects of promotion and you discover that your predecessor was in the job for ten years then do they speak with forked tongue?

■ **Before leaving today would it be in order for me to have a look around?** This question conveys enthusiasm and is a message of *intent*. It is also another 'no lose' question. For security reasons they may say that it is not possible, but at least you asked. It really is amazing how frequently people are offered, and accept, a job without seeing where they will be spending the next three to five years.

■ **If I were to join the company where might *you* see me in three to five years time?** A useful one to ask, particularly if they had previously asked you 'where do you see yourself in five years time?' This is one way of finding out whether you gave the right answer!

■ **What would you see as my priorities in this job?** A way of establishing what they see as the major problems.

Remember that they are employing you either to resolve existing problems or to prevent them from happening.

■ **Any question about an aspect of their operation in which you would not be directly involved.** On the whole, jop applicants become very myopic or blinkered in terms of the 'raison dêtre' of the company. They show an interest in their specific function but display no awareness of the overall objective of the organization. If your specific role would be in manufacturing then ask something about the marketing or distribution side.

■ **On what criteria will you judge my success in the job?** Should you be offered the job and you accept it then at some point in the future they will make a judgment on you. Far better to establish beforehand the criteria on which they will make such a judgment.

■ **To whom would I be directly accountable?** Or more importantly, 'Will I have an opportunity of meeting this person?' More often than not that person will be in on the meeting or at a subsequent meeting. However, don't assume that this will be the case. It is not a good idea (for either party) for you to accept a job without meeting the boss.

■ **I have enjoyed our discussion and am confident that I can do the job, do you have any reservations at all about my suitability?** Another 'no lose' question. Your competitors won't ask it, they will want to get out while the going is good and don't want to hear bad news. You will not be afraid for them to voice an 'objection to the sale'. If they can think of a reason why you might not get the job offer (or a second meeting) then you must make them tell you. This is your *last chance* to counter that objection – you can't do it once you have gone through the door. If they have a problem then *don't leave them with it* because they will still have it after you have left. A likely response is for them to say 'Well, I have other people to see and I don't want to make a pre-emptive decision but you appear to be a strong candidate and no real objection comes to mind'. In which case they are more psychologically disposed to offering you the job or a further meeting.

■ **When will I hear from you?** Get a commitment from them. Don't be fobbed off by a dismissive 'You will be hearing from us in due course'. Ask what the next stage is and when you might expect to hear. Once that date has passed you are justified in chasing them up. Failure to do this is a sure-fire way to lose control of your campaign and you can lose *weeks* just waiting to hear.

### Before the meeting – some additional tips

■ **If they telephone to arrange a time for the meeting do not say immediately that you are available at their suggested time and date.** Your diary is full and it is quite likely that you will need to re-arrange something. Get back to them after you have made the re-arrangement and confirm the appointment. It is not in your interest to give them the impression that you have time on your hands, but there *are* dangers in playing 'hard to get' so don't overdo it.

■ **Research the company, particularly if they declined to send you any information.** The question 'What do you know about us?' is *extremely* common and more often than not elicits a weak response from candidates. If on paper you are a 'possible' as opposed to a 'probable' then being able to answer this question will promote you into the ranks of the 'probables' in one fell swoop. If there is one thing that irritates employers most of all it is seeing candidates who have not had the initiative, courtesy and enthusiasm to find out something about the organization they are hoping to work for. *What* you find out is not important (unless you are establishing that they are on a sound financial footing), that you *did* find out something is of the utmost importance.

■ ***Never* turn down a meeting.** Even if you don't want the job and even if you don't want to work for them (then why apply in the first place?) you are making another personal contact. You also need the practice – improving your performance at meetings such as this is a cumulative learning experience. In addition, it is by no means unusual to find yourself at a meeting discussing a job *other* than the one you applied for. If you are clearly too good for the job it will soon be apparent to them and if you are performing well they may offer you something better. One thing is sure, if they do have other needs you will only find out by turning up.

■ **Your *goal* is to make them offer you the job – only then are you in a position to accept or reject**. During the course of the meeting the job may become less attractive to you. *Maintain* your enthusiasm for the company – if you become negative they won't offer you anything better. Under the pressure and stress of these meetings you are not best placed to make pre-emptive decisions about whether you want the job – problems may arise which seem insurmountable at the meetings but which pale into insignificance subsequently. Many candidates come away wishing that they had been more positive about a certain point which seemed intractable during the meeting, but which in hindsight is not a problem at all. Until you have the offer in writing you have no decision to make.

■ **Remember the 'accountability factor'.** We have already seen that the over-riding need of all recruiters is to keep their job – not give you one. This is particularly important at initial meetings. You may be seen initially by someone who is *not* the decision-maker in the sense that they can offer you the job. They will be a decision-maker of sorts: they can say 'No you will not get this job and I will not be recommending you for a second interview'. This initial interviewer is always accountable to someone else and *must* be able to justify their decision. They can only do so if you present them with enough evidence and reassure them that if they select you for a second meeting then *you will not let them down*. If you get a good rapport going you can virtually say this to them. You are telling them what they *really* want to hear.

■ **Don't worry about interview nerves unless you are nervous for all the wrong reasons.** Your competitors are likely to be nervous because they are totally unprepared. *You* should be 'nervous' because you want all your preparatory work to be reflected in your performance.

■ **Maintain your self-respect.** So-called 'stress techniques' were once quite fashionable but less so these days. However, you may come across certain individuals who try to intimidate, either because they have read all the old books on 'interviewing' or, more likely, because it is simply in their nature to be that way. You can terminate the meeting any time you like. You are busy and after all may not want to work with an organization which employs such methods. On the other hand you may wish to go along with it to test your technique. If you come away from any meeting having left your self-respect behind it will surely have an adverse effect on your performance at subsequent meetings. This is the only occasion when it is in order to make a decision before being offered the job.

- **The worst advice you can get is to 'be yourself'.** This doesn't mean that you have to submerge your natural character and personality. It does mean reminding yourself that the 'interview' is a business meeting. Go wearing your 'business hat' and not your 'social hat'. To a greater or lesser degree most people, particularly those in positions of authority, have to 'role play' ie behave in the working environment in a different manner from the one they use socially. Problems will arise when they play the wrong role. A professional boxer may be a very pleasant chap outside the ring but his trainer would not say 'It's fight night tonight but just go in the ring and be yourself'.

Finally, remember that at the meeting all candidates are equal. Successful applicants may well be better qualified but that is not why they get the job offer. Job offers are achieved by those who sell themselves best at the meeting. If selection were based solely on things like qualifications, age and experience then there would be little point in seeing anyone. It is not purely a question of whether the recruiter *likes* you – that would be too simplistic. They are looking to see if you will fit in with the organization and whether you are likely to get on with the people for and with whom you will be working.

Their decision will be based upon a visual and aural impression of you, and if you can score well on those points it can off-set any deficiencies you may have in terms of qualifications, age or experience. On paper you may only be a 'possible' but if you sell yourself well and the 'probable' doesn't, you will get the offer.

## 50 predictable interview questions to prepare for

1. How was your journey?
2. Tell me about yourself?
3. What do you know about us?
4. What do you look for in a job?
5. Why does this job interest you?
6. Why are you leaving your present employer?
7. Why did you stay with them so long?
8. You seem to have done a lot of job-hopping – why?
9. We were really looking for a younger/older person?
10. What is your greatest strength?
11. What is your greatest weakness?
12. Where do you see yourself in five years time?
13. What would you describe as your greatest achievement?
14. What was your biggest mistake?
15. What major problems did you encounter in your last job?
16. What did you do to overcome them?
17. Are you having discussions with other organizations?
18. How does this job compare?
19. What does success mean to you?
20. Are you ambitious?
21. Would you say that you had an aggressive management style?
22. How would you describe your management style?
23. What qualities do you look for in a good manager?
24. Do you prefer working on your own or in a team?
25. If you could choose any job what would it be?
26. What are your long-term career aims?
27. What was the main weakness of your last boss?
28. Has your career developed as you would have liked?
29. Would you be prepared to re-locate?
30. Have you ever failed in any job you have tried to do?
31. How would you describe your relationship with your subordinates?
32. How do you motivate them?

33. Would you accept this job if I offered it to you?
34. How important is money to you?
35. Why haven't you found a job yet?
36. Why did you not pursue 'A' levels/a degree?
37. You are lacking in specific experience for this job.
38. What can you offer us?
39. Do you have a pension?
40. What is your present salary?
41. What salary are you seeking?
42. Why did they make *you* redundant?
43. Do you ever have doubts about your ability to do a job?
44. What do you do in your spare time?
45. What makes a good leader?
46. What leadership qualities do you possess?
47. Who did your CV for you?
48. If the interests of your boss and your staff conflict, with whom would you tend to side?
49. Are you sure that this job is good enough for you?
50. Do you regard it as a weakness to 'blow your top'?

## During the meeting

> 'Now you get down on your knees
> And fiddle with your rosaries,
> Bow your head with great respect and
> Genuflect, genuflect, genuflect.'
>
> Tom Lehrer

This supplicatory attitude might be *de rigeur* for an interview at the Vatican but generally speaking no employer respects a fawning sychophant. If you *must* insist on bowing, scraping and general toadying then do wait until *after* you have got the job. Do not be kept waiting for more than 15 minutes after your appointed time – at least not without an explanation from someone. These meetings do have a nasty habit of over-running and this is not necessarily a problem, but don't put up with shabby treatment, it's an indication of how you might be treated when working for them.

You will arrive 15 minutes early and if you are offered a drink accept if you wish. If you are not offered anything until five minutes before your appointed time then it might be wise to decline the offer. Should you accept under those circumstances you will be burdened with a hot drink just as the recruiter appears, seemingly from nowhere. You will not know whether to leave it or take it with you and if they don't advise you accordingly you will be off to a shaky start.

If you are laden down with overcoat, briefcase, umbrella etc leave your right arm free from such encumberances for the time when a handshake is proferred. Should you have to extricate your hand from beneath a pile of personal effects then you will be psychologically off-balance at the critical moment – and all because you are physically off-balance. Make sure you give a *firm* handshake – a limp or bone-crushing handshake can have a most profound effect upon whoever happens to be on the receiving end.

*Smile* and greet people *by name*. Remember that *they* are likely to be nervous too. Recruiters never know *what* is going to come through the door and those first two minutes are very important. Until you prove otherwise you are likely to be seen as a threat and the smile does much to dispel such fear.

Go along with any 'small talk' – this is all part of the initial 'jousting' and a professional will try to put you at your ease – but refrain from telling them that you had a lousy journey and couldn't for the life of you find their premises. If your home is some way away from the potential place of work they may be concerned about your ability to get there should they offer you the job, in which case telling them how awful the journey was can only confirm their fears.

It is quite important to display a sense of humour but do be careful about this. Avoid making jokes or displaying a frivolous manner. Laughter can be alarmingly close to hysteria. Maintain eye contact. A surprisingly high number of even executive-level people have a problem with this. There is much in the saying 'the eyes have it' and it is easy to come across as 'shifty' if you keep staring at your shoes. This may be no more than shyness but this in itself can be a negative factor if they are particularly seeking someone with confidence. On the other hand don't stare them out – you don't want them to think that they are in the presence of a homicidal maniac.

Know when to keep quiet. If you feel that you have dealt with a particular point effectively do not continue talking if they have paused. A five second pause may feel like five minutes to you but sit tight – don't be afraid of the silence. The pause is a technique often used by professionals to get people to say imprudent things. Amateurs will do it because they do not know what they are going to say next – it is nonetheless effective.

Be *in control* of the meeting. It is often said that *they* should be in control and by and large this is correct – you must not be overbearing. Being in control means knowing those points you want to get across and devising ways in which to do so. This highlights the importance of preparation. The dangerous questions at these meetings are not always the initial questions but those 'follow-up' questions that arise from your answers to the initial questions! To really be in control you must develop the ability to keep one step ahead.

It is a question of saying 'If they ask me *that*, what answer should I give?' and then taking it one step further by saying 'Well, if I give that answer what follow-up question might they come up with?' It doesn't require a quantum leap of the imagination to then say 'Well, what question would I like them to follow up with?' It will naturally be a question which allows you to get across yet another selling point. *You* are in control but are doing it in such a way that they still think they are.

Try to recognize *the point at which you have made the sale*. In every meeting there is an optimum time within which they will have made some kind of decision. This time could be within the first five minutes (in which case the decision is likely to be a negative one) or not until two hours have elapsed. The decision reached could be 'yes', 'no' or 'maybe'. If the decision is 'yes' then any further selling on your part can prove counter-productive – many, many people have had a job offer in their pocket within an hour (if only they had known it) only to lose it by over-selling and not allowing the recruiter to wind things up. This is why you need to know how long the meeting is due to last (see page 166).

Watch out for the signals – if they start shuffling their papers together and looking anxiously at their watches then they have made a decision and want to get away. Let them. These signals, and your own judgment on how well you are performing, will determine the number and type of questions you will want to ask at the end (see pages 168–71).

---

### Hazard warning

■ Beware of the *implied job offer*. They may make all the right noises during the meeting and virtually offer you the job at the end of it, or at least strongly imply that you will get the job offer. Keep it to yourself and carry on job-hunting until you have something in writing.

In all good faith the person you are seeing may want you but is it *their* decision? The job offer may not be within their gift and *they* may have forgotten the 'accountability factor' (see page 172). There have been many, many instances where the candidate has been verbally offered the job, on the strength of which they have cancelled all other interviews, wound down their job search and stood down their personal contacts and then been asked to make a 'courtesy call' on the Managing Director (expecting no more than a 'welcome aboard' and perhaps a sherry) only to find themselves facing a two-hour grilling from the MD at the end of which, no job offer! You do not have a job offer until you have it in writing.

---

## Understanding the questions

There is an infinite number of questions which may arise at meetings – not all of which you will be able to anticipate. Some questions are formulated in such a way that the questioner can identify 'what makes you tick?' Others are more negative – designed to identify 'What stops your clock?'.

Success lies in your ability to distinguish quickly between these 'sell' and 'defend' questions and fire off the appropriate response. What follows is a selection of typical questions from each category and a brief discussion of each question. It is pointless to try and give 'stock answers' – your meetings will be unique. The intention is for you to *understand* why certain questions are asked and the sometimes hidden problems they can present.

## 'So what makes you tick?'

These are questions which do tend to give some cause for concern, but unnecessarily so since they are not inherently dangerous. They are all questions which give you an excellent opportunity to do a good selling job on yourself. Indeed, some of them are akin to being offered a blank cheque – it is amazing how few people take the trouble to fill it in.

### *'Tell me about yourself'*

This is the archetypal blank cheque question. Interpret it as if they had said 'Tell me why I should employ you'. Tell them. Don't do as your competitors do and leave this to chance – you can't cobble together a meaningful answer to this question on the spot. Don't ask them to define *what* you should talk about – they will and you won't be happy with the topic. Have *prepared* a two minute talk, the first minute of which accounts for the *relevant* details of your career to date, and the second minute of which tells them *how* that career equips you for *this* job. Two minutes is a long time. Family background, hobbies and where you go for your holidays might be interesting but are unlikely to help them reach a positive decision. Once you have this short talk prepared you will only need to adjust it for subsequent meetings – you will not need to 're-invent the wheel' every time.

### 'What are your strong points?'

Or 'What can the product do?' The strong points you relate may not be your strongest points but they will be your strongest points in relation to the job being discussed. Be specific and don't waffle on about adaptability, sense of humour or your ability to get on with people – you are not a contestant for *Miss World*.

### 'Why have you applied for this job?'

You have presumably applied because you have the skills to do the job well. Outline what you see as their needs and reiterate how you can fulfil them. Your reasons for applying must emphasize what you can *contribute* and not what you can *take*. Let your competitors stress what the job can give them in terms of salary, job satisfaction or career progression. Try to imagine the questioner repeating your answer to their superior. Would they feel happier to say that your interest in the job lies in the fact that you have the skills/experience they are seeking or because it can give you what you are seeking?

### 'Where do you see yourself in two/five years time?'

Keep an open mind. Don't pin yourself down to a specific and perhaps mythical job title – your goal may be unrealistic or even threatening to *their* feeling of security. Make the point that as long as you are getting results, making a contribution and learning new skills then you see yourself still working for *them*. This is a particularly useful response if they might have perceived you as being a 'job-hopper'. Stating a specific and unrealistic objective will alert them to the fact that they could not satisfy your career ambitions.

### 'What do you know about us?'

*What* you know is not so important as the fact that you know *something*. If this question comes up it will do so early on in the meeting. If you know nothing then although they will carry on with the meeting they will mentally have dismissed you. If they *don't* ask and you have done your homework well, it would be a waste for you to leave without having made the point that you have gone to the trouble to find out about them. Be prepared then to get this across when it is your turn to ask questions, eg 'I notice from your Annual Report that next year you are expanding into Europe. Can you tell me how that might affect this job?' The question you ask may not be as important as the fact that they now know you read their report.

### '*What is your greatest achievement?*'
Now you may consider your greatest achievement was winning the North West Area Tango Dancing Championship in 1978, but this would elicit not a few yawns if you were being vetted for General Manager of XYZ Road Haulage Company. Be prepared to go for a lesser achievement if it is more relevant to their needs.

### '*Are you ambitious?*'
Be careful. This *could* be a dangerous question if you are getting on in years and your career to date shows a distinct lack of progression. Generally speaking, employers like to see people who aren't content to just stand still. A professional should always be looking for the next challenge, new problems to solve, improvements to be made. This need not mean that you want to be Managing Director – but it could be dangerous to indicate that you don't. It could imply that you lack confidence. Distinguish between ability and *desire* – ambition need not mean that you want to progress up the career ladder.

## So what stops your clock?
Other questions are designed to probe any weaknesses you may be perceived as having, and all can be interpreted as 'Tell me why I shouldn't employ you'. They are 'objections to the sale' which must be recognized when they appear and then countered positively. They are drawn from a common kitty of 'fast ball' questions that experienced recruiters are fond of

dipping into. For the most part, being prepared will ensure that you come through them unscathed.

### 'What is your greatest weakness?'

Not unlike being offered a poisoned chalice. Decline the offer, not by denying the existence of any weaknesses (we all have them) but by giving them a weakness which can be interpreted as a strength. By any stretch of the imagination this is a tough question so, even though you know how to counter it, pause, stare philosophically out of the window and then respond, perhaps with: 'This is a difficult question because we don't see ourselves as others see us, but my colleagues do sometimes accuse me of being too demanding – nevertheless, we do achieve results and maintain a good team spirit'.

### 'What problems did you have to overcome in your last job?'

A good question to get and there is no mileage at all in your denying the existence of any problems. Of course they will not be problems that you should have anticipated, least of all caused, and neither will you be interested in apportioning blame. Any cited problems must not reflect badly upon your previous employer. Make sure that the problem *was* overcome, that you were instrumental in overcoming it and that it required a range of skills to do so.

### 'Do you have an aggressive management style?'

A 'closed' question which is not particularly useful but they may have a reason for putting it this way. Certainly, one's style of management is always of great interest. Are they seeking someone with a tough management style? The previous job-holder may have been too aggressive – they won't want another one. On the other hand they might not want the silent type who manages by consensus. If it is unclear what they are seeking your only certainty of staying in the game is to hedge your bets: 'I believe I am adaptable enough to change my style depending on the situation and the person. Some people respond well to a robust approach but others need encourage-ment to perform well. Good managers should know what makes their staff tick and manage accordingly.'

If it subsequently becomes clear that they are demanding a style of management you cannot deliver, then consider carefully the wisdom of accepting the position. But only when you have the offer do you need to make that choice.

*'I understand that you were made redundant from your last job?'*
'Yes, unfortunately'. Even if *your job* was made redundant it would be foolish to acquiesce so meekly. Such an answer implies that regret, if not resentment, is being harboured. How about 'Over the past two years quite a few jobs have gone. We thought we were over the worst but now a further dozen jobs must go and mine is one of them. However, I do see this as a great opportunity to move my career along and use my skills within an organization such as yours'? It is implicit in this answer that redundancy relates to the job and not the person, that more than one job is affected and that the situation is being viewed positively by you.

*'You don't have any experience of marketing do you?'*
Remember, if it was *really* a problem they wouldn't have asked you to the meeting. However, it is not good enough to respond by saying 'No, I'm afraid I don't'. How about 'I relish the challenge of taking on the marketing. I can satisfy most of your needs and I am looking to broaden my experience. The marketing role very much attracts me and because I am adaptable and quick to learn I really don't foresee a problem'? This answer emphasizes suitability in all other respects, demonstrates enthusiasm and ambition and gets across two other selling points. Make your 'weaknesses' work for you.

*'Why did you stay so long with one company?'*
Accusations of inertia are scant reward for years of 'loyalty' to a former employer. If your career has not moved on apace with

that employer then you could be in trouble as we discovered in Part 1. If it has then there is no problem. You might say, 'They were a good company to work for and as you will see from my CV I didn't stand still. They were quick to recognize and encourage ability and I never felt the need to develop my career outside the company.'

*'You seem to have done a lot of job-hopping – why?'*
It may seem as though you can't win! If you have moved from one employer to another in a series of unrelated and undistinguished moves then again you can have a problem – the rationale for making each move will be carefully dissected. If they have been reasonably logical and progressive career moves then you simply need to turn the previous answer on its head: 'I don't like to stand still for too long. I have always found that in order to progress my career at the speed I want to go I have had to move outside the company to do it – I would naturally prefer to expand my career within the same organization – do you feel that I will have this opportunity with your company?'

## 'We were looking for someone a little younger – do you think this will be a problem?'

Again, remember that if they *really* felt age was a big deal then you wouldn't have got to this stage: your date of birth is on your sales literature and they wouldn't waste their time. Then why should they ask the question? Because although they do not necessarily see age as a problem *they need to find out if you do*. If you react aggressively or go on the defensive then they will know that they have attacked your Achilles Heel. You will be transmitting signals which indicate to them (albeit perhaps unfairly) that you do see it as a problem, in which case it will be one.

Respond with surprise, enthusiasm and a smile: 'not at all, I feel as young now as I did 20 years ago. I am fit, healthy and enthusiastic and I mix in very well with people even younger than myself – no problem'. They will be only too pleased to pass this information on to their superior (the 'accountability factor' again).

However, it is ineffective if your voice is saying these words but your body is saying the opposite. Chronological age is rarely a problem in itself – which is why employers will often give the benefit of the doubt and agree to see people who are 'over the age limit'.

### 'What was your greatest mistake?'

Like all questions, this is not a problem providing you give it some thought beforehand. Whatever you say must show you in a good light. There is no point at all in quoting a mistake which was avoidable, your fault and disastrous in its consequences. Not pursuing educational qualifications can be seen as a mistake but if you have done well regardless this speaks highly of you. As with 'lack of experience', you can, with a little thought, make an apparently negative factor work in your favour.

### 'Do you prefer working on your own or as a member of a team?'

If you know whether the job in question is autonomous or dependent upon team work then this might determine your response. If you don't know then you could be 'damned if you do and damned if you don't'. Do not allow yourself to be forced into making a choice between two alternatives. Why should you have a preference? You might say. 'I'm not sure that I have a preference as such. In my present job I enjoy working closely with a team but in my previous job I was quite autonomous and I thoroughly enjoyed the responsibility'.

### 'If I were able to offer you any job what would it be – what do you really want to do?'

A strange question you might think but nevertheless quite common. It is an effective way of establishing what career ambitions have not been realized and is based on the assumption that no one is doing what they really want to do – that we are all in some way compromising. Let your competitors bemoan the fact that they really wanted to be engine drivers or ballerinas – the questioner will then be interested to find out what stopped them achieving it. There is a two-word answer to the question: 'This job'. Any other answer implies that the job you are discussing is second best.

### 'Why haven't you found a job yet?'

The longer you are in the job market the less desirable you become. This on its own is an excellent reason for managing an intensive job-search campaign. If other employers are showing no sign of taking you on then there must be something wrong with the product mustn't there? Not necessarily. Just because you have no job people should not presume that you haven't been offered one. Don't let them get away with this. Say something like 'Well, I am being selective about my choice of job. I could have accepted others but, *unlike this one*, I did not see them as being good career moves.' If you *have* declined other offers all well and good. If you haven't, then think very carefully before indicating as much.

### 'Are you having discussions with any other organization?'

Of course you are. If you are not then there is something seriously wrong with your campaign planning. You are not obliged to tell them *who* you are talking to but it may be in your interests to let them know if you are having meaningful discussion with a prestigious company, particularly if it happens to be one of their competitors. They will then be anxious not to lose you. If this question arises at an initial meeting then it is certainly in your interests to let them know that you have reached the second stage with other employers. This will indicate to them that if they want you they had better get a move on. It will also reassure them to know that other organizations agree with them that you are worth seeing a second time.

A negative answer to this question will almost certainly weaken your position.

## Negotiating the package – or 'if you pay peanuts you get monkeys'

Remember how important it is to move away from the traditional view that you will be negotiating *salary*. Your first step is to work out precisely what your present job is worth to you. Break it down into its component parts, eg salary, company car, mileage allowance, free/subsidized meals, profit share, private health, pension etc. Average out any bonuses you may have received. The final figure you come to will probably surprise you. As you naturally want to improve upon this, the figure will represent the total remuneration package (TRP) below which you are not prepared to go.

Any job offer must then, in financial terms, be compared to this. In arriving at your present TRP you will probably have discovered that the computations can be quite complex. Because of this it is not necessarily a good idea to negotiate the package at the meeting itself. The best time to negotiate is when you have a written job offer which details the breakdown of the package they are offering – you can then compare the two in the comfort of your own home and not during the pressurized and stressful meeting itself.

If you have achieved your objective of multiple job offers you will be in a strong position to negotiate. Not only can you use *this* job offer as a lever to speed up the progress of other applications but you can also use *better* offers to improve *this* offer if it is really the *right job*.

Ideally you should set up an 'auction' situation whereby you *discreetly* play one off against the other. This *can* become very competitive – the more organizations that are after your services the more desirable you become, although this may depend very much on the uniqueness of your skills.

**Hazard warning**

■ If you are confident and competent this can be the most enjoyable and rewarding aspect of the job search. If you are *not*, it can be disastrous. You owe it to yourself to get the best deal that you can but it takes some skill (and nerve) to do it well. It is very easy to be 'too clever by half' and many employers are not willing to be 'held to ransom'. Certainly negotiate but don't overdo it and be sensitive to their situation.

## But what if they raise the salary issue at the meeting?

This is almost certain to happen, if not at the first meeting then at the second. How you proceed will depend upon a number of factors:

■ Their understanding of your present salary/ package and your understanding of what they might be offering
■ The *timing* ie *when* they choose to raise the subject
■ *How* they choose to raise the subject

Prior to the meeting you should have given them no indication at all regarding your present remuneration. If the job was advertised they may have given an indication in terms of a figure (useful) or merely said 'attractive' or 'negotiable' (largely meaningless). If they are aware of your present remuneration this puts you at a disadvantage because they will negotiate from there. If they are not then they may feel that it is appropriate to ask you. It isn't.

*'What is your present salary?'*
Here we come to the issue of *timing*. If this question is asked early in the interview you should not discuss salary at all – *never*

*discuss the price before you have made the sale.* You may wish to respond thus: 'I would prefer to talk in terms of the overall package as I find that basic salaries can be misleading – but would you mind if we come back to it later, I would rather tell you what I can offer your company?'

You have now side-stepped the issue in a reasonable manner, indicated that you are not going to be pushed around, made the point about salary versus package and tempted them to ask you what it is you are offering.

The meeting will now progress and you are telling them all the good things about yourself which are making you more attractive to them.

If the question is asked towards the end of the meeting, say something like: 'I would prefer to talk in terms of the overall package as I find that basic salaries can be misleading. I enjoy the usual benefits one might expect for someone with my skills and experience ('at my level', 'in my position' etc). I am naturally seeking to improve on my present position and it would be helpful to me if you could give me an indication of what salary and range of benefits you might be thinking of offering?'

This has told them absolutely nothing and fired the question straight back at them. Hopefully, they will then go on to give you an indication of what they are thinking of offering. Whatever sums they divulge it is important that you remain impassive but maintain a degree of enthusiasm. You could say, 'On that basis I certainly feel that we are not wasting each other's time. May I suggest that we leave it there for now – should you wish to make me an offer in writing I can then do my sums and come back to you?'

Once you have the offer in writing do your sums. If their offer is wildly in excess of what you were seeking then *don't be greedy*. If you will be worse off, then start negotiating. This negotiation may be done over the telephone. Let us assume that their offer is £1,000 short of your *target* (not necessarily your present package). Perhaps you could say, 'Thank you very much for your offer. I am certain that we are right for each other and I would be delighted to accept. However, having done my sums carefully it's clear that I would in fact be worse off by about £1,750 – is there room for negotiation?'

Now either there is room for negotiation or there isn't. If there is then you may receive £1,750, £1,500 or £1,000, any of which would be acceptable to you. They would be unlikely to go below £1,000 more. If there is no room for negotiation you will still have a decision to make – take it or leave it. (This decision may of course hinge upon the time when the salary/package is due for review by the company.)

### 'What sort of salary are you seeking?'

This is a marginally better way for the issue to be raised – at least they are not being impertinent enough to ask for your present salary. The previous rules on timing apply. If it is raised towards the end of the meeting you may wish to respond thus: 'I would prefer to talk in terms of the overall package as I find that basic salaries can be misleading. For the moment I am keeping a fairly open mind – for the right job the remuneration may not be the deciding factor. However, I am seeking to maximize my earning potential and, naturally, improve on my present position – whenever you consider it appropriate it would be helpful to me if you could indicate what package you are thinking of offering.'

Negotiating salary is not an exact science but you can lower their opinion of you if you fail to negotiate. On balance it is far better to pitch your remuneration requirements at *too high* a level than *too low*. They may try to 'beat the price down' if they want you but if you set it too low they won't want you. You may soon get the impression from them that they are prepared to offer the job to the least expensive applicant and that for them 'salary' will be the deciding factor. They may raise red herrings by talking about the 'going rate for the job'. This is completely irrelevant. At the end of the day either they want the job done *well* or they want it done *cheap*.

---

**Hazard warning**

■ Don't assume that the salary issue is being raised when in fact it isn't. A very oblique way of sounding you out on your attitudes towards finance is for them to pose the rather enigmatic question, 'How important is money to you?' A typical, and dangerous response is for candidates to *deny* the importance of it by saying 'Well, it is fairly important but there are more important things like job satisfaction and career development – salary isn't the 'be all and end all'. This is a weak response and will do you no favours when they do raise the salary issue. Much better for you to take it out of the salary context and remember that they are a profit-making organization, or at least (if public sector) have to keep within budgets. So you might say something like, 'Money is very important. The only reason you exist as a company is to make a profit. I expect all employees to have an awareness of the importance of money – whatever our role we must be cost-effective and profit-conscious.'

---

## After the meeting

Most job applicants come away from the meeting, breathe a sigh of relief and then sit back and wait for the result. This is no good at all – the game is still on. What action can you take to enhance your case yet further? By now you may have guessed it – yes, the good old follow-up letter! This will be a very brief letter, the aim of which is to:

■ Thank them for their time
■ Say how much you enjoyed the discussion
■ Confirm your interest in the position, and *perhaps*
■ Give them further evidence of your suitability which did not come out during the meeting

Again, sending such a letter is not an 'optional extra'. It is essential that you send it because it really can make the difference between whether you or a competitor gets the job offer. It is certainly not 'too late' to supply them with further information – after all, it is in both your interests that they reach the right decision and if they don't have all the facts this may not happen. However, don't labour the point – they may think you are desperate. The letter is a courteous and businesslike end to the proceedings.

## Review your performance

Following a meeting, have you ever received a rejection letter which *really* told you why you were unsuccessful? It is very unlikely that you have. Receipt of such a letter would initially be somewhat disappointing but good quality feedback does give something to build on. In practice, of course, employers are busy people and have no time to de-brief candidates. Even if this were not so they would have no desire to run the risk of being hurtful.

In the likely absence of useful feedback from the company, it is vitally important that you de-brief *yourself* immediately after the meeting. Do this quickly, because your powers of recall will diminish with time. The aim of the 'de-brief' is to assess if you came across as well as you are capable of doing, ie was the recruiter receiving favourably the signals you were transmitting? How well did you perform? If it went well ask yourself 'why?' If you did it once you can do it again. A good performance is normally a reflection of the preparing, rehearsing and practising that you did beforehand. If parts of it went badly then, again, ask yourself 'why?' Perhaps it was a question you hadn't anticipated? Be ready for it next time. Perhaps your attitude wasn't quite right? Did you arrive at the meeting in the right frame of mind? If you crossed the threshold up to your ears in 'angst' and riddled with all manner of doubts this would immediately have communicated itself to the other party.

If you look good and feel good then you will probably perform well. 'Looking the part' is often ignored by candidates

– not surprisingly, as this is largely a matter of luck. It is not always feasible to skulk around outside the premises the day before in an effort to determine what the employees coming and going are wearing. However, many organizations have an identifiable 'corporate image' which is often reflected in dress. *If you arrive at the meeting looking as if you already work there then you are more likely to end up doing so.* We do of course have our off days. Preparation normally pays off but you can't win 'em all (hence the need for multiple meetings). On the other hand, don't be too quick to put a poor performance down to dodgy bio-rhythms or Jupiter's unfavourable alignment with Mars.

### How to turn rejections into job offers

After an apparently good meeting, and particularly after reaching the shortlist stage, receiving a rejection letter can indeed be a bitter blow. More so if you have *not* planned your campaign and have no other offers on the horizon. The question is, what do you do about it? Yes, even at this stage the game is still on and the position is recoverable. If you reached the shortlist of, say, four people it is more than likely that any one of you could have done the job. At this stage, and particularly if their selection process has been methodical and professional, their final decision may be quite arbitrary and if they could they would probably offer all of you a job. They can't do this so three candidates are going to be disappointed. One candidate is going to be very happy – or are they? Any one of a number of things can (and do) now go wrong:

- Will the successful candidate accept the job? If they are doing their job-hunting as well as you are doing yours then *they* will have other offers to consider. They may have made all the right noises but will turn the offer down at the last moment
- Even after accepting the job the successful candidate can change his/her mind if a better offer comes up

■ Even after *starting* the job, that candidate (now employee) can leave quickly for a number of reasons

Apart from anything else the company may have made a mistake. Many candidates do well at the meetings but the employers soon discover that they have made a bad choice.

If such a problem develops (and it frequently does) the employer is very unlikely to go through the recruiting process all over again. Their most likely move will be to go back to the shortlist. *Who* out of those three 'rejected' will they approach? They will nearly always go back to the candidate who had the foresight to send them a conciliatory letter indicating that such an approach would be welcome. Why? Because it is difficult to go back to people one has rejected – the employer will grab at any olive branch. Your letter is that olive branch.

Your letter should be brief, something like the following:

'I am naturally disappointed to have been unsuccessful this time. However, I thoroughly enjoyed our discussion and am most impressed by your plans for the future. Because of this I would be very pleased to receive an approach from you should the situation change, or indeed if a similar position arises within the next few weeks.'

You may find you don't feel like writing such a letter immediately on receipt of their letter. But remember that you must never give up on a job even when you appear to have lost it. A seven-line letter can get you a job.

## Assessing the job offer

On receipt of a job offer read the small print. Is the job being offered the one you discussed at the meeting? This might seem an odd question but it is surprising how different it can look in black and white. Check that the remuneration package is in line with what may have been indicated at the meeting. Are the benefits detailed? Holidays acceptable? Do they provide an 'outplacement' service should redundancy rear its ugly head? (You can have such a service written into your contract.) Is the relocation package (if any) clearly detailed? Are reporting structures clearly outlined? Now is the time to iron out any anomolies and negotiate terms and conditions. One thing is for sure, you can't do it after you have started the job – the game is then over.

Above all, is it the *right* job? Your campaign has been a long and testing journey – it would be a pity to blow it at this stage. Now is the time for you to return to the Self Analysis Exercise that you completed in Chapter Three. In accepting this offer would you be fulfilling your personal needs, or might you be compromising in any way? Look again at the results you obtained on the matrix (page 45). You have two lists – 'Skills' and 'Motivators'. Remember that in descending order these were the skills that you *enjoyed* using. Will the job on offer allow you to carry on using these skills? You also separated out those skills that you did *not* enjoy – does the job require you to use *those* skills? If so the alarm bells should start ringing – is it the *wrong* job?

The job may satisfy your requirements in terms of the skills you would be employing but are the motivators present? If they are not then the job may not be so enjoyable *even if you are using the same skills*. For example, a recurrent motivator may have been 'working for a small organization'. If the job offer comes from a large multi-national, job satisfaction *may* be diminished.

Does the job offer you anything *new*? Here we return to the 'fifth law of personal career management' – your next move will be on your CV forever. If you accept this job how will it look on your CV when you are ready to make your next positive career move?

## The job offer 'Litmus test'

■ Let us assume for a moment that your previous job became redundant and you were thrown unceremoniously into the job market. You now have a job offer and may well be tempted to grab it most gratefully. But first ask yourself one simple question: 'If my previous job had not gone, and I was still in work, would I have been tempted by this new job?' If it would not have tempted you from a position of strength, ie employment, what is the logic of accepting it from a position of relative weakness, ie unemployment?

You may 'rationalize' that although it is an unattractive offer it will provide you with an income of sorts and 'tide you over' while you search for something better. This is whistling in the dark. In practice you will not continue your job search. Your first six months in the job, however 'lightweight' it is, will be spent on a 'learning curve' and this will leave no time for job-hunting. By the time six months have passed you will have made new friends and (if you dropped your salary) become accustomed to a lower standard of living – inertia will have set in.

# CONCLUSION

The purpose of this book can best be summed up by relating an experience I had when advising a job-hunting client for the first time. He was intelligent, personable, well-dressed and had in the past achieved much. But he had not been *in control* of his career. Complacency had set in for many of the reasons discussed in Part 1, until one day the music stopped and his chair was removed. Despite applying for many jobs he achieved no success and was becoming increasingly despondent. At an appropriate point in our discussion I tactfully suggested that he was perhaps suffering from an inferiority complex. After a moment's thought he replied 'You are wrong you know, it's not a complex – I *am* inferior!' Now inferior he clearly was not but his somewhat perverse reply indicated that his mind had gone into a 'self-destruct' mode because of his lack of success in the job market.

Constant rejection can lead to a dangerous cocktail of emotions: anger, shame, embarrassment, guilt, frustration – all negative emotions which become the enemy of self-confidence, optimism and the will to succeed. The 'knock on' effect is that these emotions are reflected in our *attitude* towards the career-management process itself. Our *thoughts* must dictate our *actions*. When we are in a negative situation, ie the wrong job or no job at all, our thoughts, and subsequently our actions, become negative. The result is that inertia sets in and we literally settle for 'the best of a bad job'. Potential employers will receive these negative signals and press the reject button. Continual rejection leads to a feeling of hopelessness until the fear of failure gives way to the fear of trying. This is why some job-seekers drop out of the market altogether.

Career management and job search is a game, albeit a serious one. You are now aware of the rules of this game and as such have the means to move forward with confidence, optimism and a *positive mental attitude*. All games require an element of luck but only the losers sit around waiting to 'get lucky'. Make your own luck by putting the rules into practice. The 'window of opportunity' is open – step on through and get the job you deserve.

# INDEX